Arundhadhi Niyamam

Screenplay to Success.....

R. Senthil kumar

ISBN

Paperback 979-8-89588-650-2

Hardcase 979-8-89699-308-7

CONTENTS

INTRODUCTION

Before I could elucidate the purpose of this book, I would request you to kindly understand the below learning methodology which can be applied to impact business drive and impart education in schools, colleges, and management institutes. The learning philosophy is called

'Arundhdhi Niyamam'.

Arundhdhi and Vashista are two twin stars. The significance of this particular twin-star is they chase each other in a circular orbit, whereas in most of the other twin stars, one will be stationary and the other will orbit around in a circular path. After every marriage, the newlywed couple is asked to see the stars in the sky to live the way the twin stars exist. The book that you hold in hand has no relation with the husband-wife bondage or the marriage ritual. But is based on the Arundhati Niyamam - Niyamam is a rule or discipline based on the context. This teaching methodology, which is used to refer to the location of Arundhdhi and Vashista in the sky, has great significance to this book. I have used Arundhdhi Niyamam to explain the leadership, management, and business philosophies of excellence. Let me explain the Arundhdhi Niyamam-Philosophy.

To show the star they refer to the nearest well-known object. After completing the marriage ceremony, the pandit will take the newlywed couple outside the marriage hall and point his fingers, "Dear couple, look at the yellow tall building. Now look at the big red tower behind that. To the left of the tower, can you see the temple gopuram? Next to the gopuram, look at the mountain on the left side of the temple gopuram. Look above the second peak of the mountain, you will find the star twinkling. That is Arundadhi star (natchatiram). They are twin stars but will be seen as one from earth as they chase each other in a circular orbit at a distance."

Long story short – The pandit uses Arundhdhi niyamam (learning methodology), taking them from the known to the unknown. If you directly show them the stars among the other stars, they may miss it or it will be a probability game. When you use Arundathi niyamam, it will be a sure shot accomplishment of the task. The brain will find it comfortable to move from the known to the unknown rather than directly jumping to the unknown.

To explain the unknown, always start with the well-known. In this book, we show the well-known personalities and movie scenes from which we take their awareness to the unknown leadership and management philosophy. A fun-filled journey of perspectives which will help us learn a rewarding experience.

Movies and cricket are the two big religions in India, well-known and interesting examples. We shall use them to learn business and leadership lessons. The current generation requires inspiration. They do it if it feels good, no right or wrong for them. Let's help them to feel good about doing the right things using their iconic examples in movies and stars.

Excellence is a product of inspiration. Inspire a client with a product (Sales). Inspire the team with a mission (Leadership). Inspire the organisation with systems and processes (Brand building).

The movies we saw and the feelings that moved us to connect with sales, leadership and management made our teams perform and create world-class organisations.

Especially for the execution of any strategy, very little technical cognizance but inspiration paves the way for things to result in action.

Most of us know the solution, but to execute is to inspire and connect with the team using well-known and interesting tools – Movies and cricket are such tools. This book helps you to instantly connect with your team and inspire them. The moment you mention the name of the personality, they will be able to connect with the subject and the context. Your message will enter their veins with ease.

Quality of Experience Is the Quality of Life

The area we give undivided **attention becomes the ultimate experience. We get that in a movie theatre.** Any experience where we forget the 'I' and get ourselves totally imbibed is an ultimate experience. A movie is such a great life experience. Close your eyes and think of any such experience that would be the 'Total Living'.

Any business market is VUCA (Volatility, Uncertainty, Complexity and Ambiguity). Unique thinking creates a difference in the domain of movies and business. If you are an effective business leader, you must inspire people by connecting with them on an emotional level. It's a cakewalk for you to penetrate their minds and create an impact in this world. Inspired learning will take them to new horizons of excellence. It improves performance, creates 'A' players effortlessly, and establishes a truly world-class organisation. When we use the well-known analogy, we shall hit the right chord.

"Knowing the solution is not enough, how you sell it and drive with passion to the team makes the difference."

CHAPTER - I
LESSONS FROM BAAHUBALI

LESSON – 1

BAAHUBALI A BIG SENSATION IN OUR LIFETIME

Few scenes can be used to illustrate some management lessons. I would like to share perspective on the same.

I learnt. Sorry, I felt a lot from the movie Baahubali scenes. I would like to share a few lessons which I feel will add value to us in managing business and building a team.

In the very first scene, you will find a mad elephant creating problems for the people. Running from one place to another in the market, destroying things, dominating the place to show it is very powerful. To show and prove that it can overpower anyone. This is a classic behaviour of a top performer behaving with too much attitude and defying the rules. They are good and they perform better; sometimes they may be smarter than the boss and they will start feeling that they are bigger and better than the company. Slowly, they may feel bigger than the organisation.

As a young star in the company tells those around them, "I am the only responsible person in total for my success, I am better than you, I am special, I am talented." The young talent doesn't know either the humility factor or gratitude that garners and augurs future growth. Typically success reaching ahead.

A young star performer feels, "I am a star, I am successful."

Eventually, he cannot handle success. He may display poor respect towards seniors and arrogance towards peers, displaying dereliction of duty.

In corporate, they term this person an 'Attitude Problem' when you discuss with seniors, they popularly say, "Nobody is indispensable. The company will run without them." The most common decision is to eliminate him. Do we have any other way to retain such talented stars by correcting them? Yes, the movie scene will give you the answer.

But if you look at the movie Baahubali, he will not kill the arrogant elephant. They will hit the elephant with something (Ganapathy car) that has a relation with the elephant - A Ganapathy Idol Car. Someone who has a bonding and relation alone should hit and control the star performer. Whenever you want to correct someone, establish a positive relation or use someone who had already established a positive relation with the concerned person.

Sweet slap: The one who has a relationship should scold them, scream at them, and take the bull by the horns with an intention to get him back with more inclusiveness. It is like entering a chakra vyukam. The one who knows how to come out must enter chakra vyukam in warfare; similarly, the one who knows how to console must take control.

> ***You should know how to control using power.***
>
> ***and***
>
> ***You should know how to console using love,***

Cool it with the turmeric powder (love and praise), then he will do the super project like the elephant.

This is the classic way to do. Most importantly, you try to control their ego, but you may end up destroying their aspiration and passion within the organisation.

Before this incident, the elephant and Baahubali didn't have a relationship. But after the hit, he develops a relationship. You work with them and tell them that you are tough with him because you want them to be a superstar and not just a star. Then he will execute the super project using it.

1. Things you should do - hit him with someone who has a relationship.

2. Cool him down.

3. Motivate him to do the super project.

So if you find a star performer struggling with his feelings of superiority.

Don't Eliminate Him. Just Illuminate Him.

Even in the life of the Great Superstar Rajinikanth, there were problems. He underwent a problem. Once he started making money, he got addicted to liquor, which took a toll on his career, and slowly people started to isolate him. Many leaders like Balachander, his wife Latha Rajinikanth, did this treatment with him to take him to a level of a superstar (of course with the blessings of Swami Ragavendra). So when talented people throw attitude **"Don't push him out. Just pull him up."**

Use the Problem to Raise a hero. If people are better than you, make sure that they stay in the company. We want talents, a small tweaking on their way of looking at things should be done. Removing the problem is important, not the person, because their talent is a wonderful treasure to be used and developed for the growth of the company and country.

Don't Break Them, Give Them a Breakthrough

Hit the elephant - Pacify the elephant - Develop a strong relationship - Execute the super project

LESSON NO - 2

When you find the conversation between Baahubali and Katappa, when the two parrots are feeding each other. Baahubali's mind was in a romantic mode, whereas Kattapa's mind was in foodie mode. This tells the conditioning of the mind and creating thought pattern.

Here we have a great opportunity to understand the function of the brain. Weighing less than 5% of the body but consuming more than 25% of your energy. More than 100 billion neurons.

1.	The brain will ask questions.
2.	It will seek answers.
3.	It will create meaning.
4.	It will choose to practise.

When your mind is healthy

1.	The brain will ask the right questions.
2.	It will seek the right answers.
3.	It will create the right meanings.
4.	It will choose to practise the right things..

When your mind is unhealthy

> 1. The brain will ask the wrong questions.
>
> 2. It will seek the wrong answers.
>
> 3. It will create the wrong meanings.
>
> 4. It will choose to practise the wrong things.

A beautiful story of a hunter and his friend where the hunter had a dog with a special ability to walk in water. The friend looked at it and did not comment or appreciate. The hunter broke the silence and asked, "Can you see something about the dog?" The friend replied, "Yes, it cannot swim in water."

The friend chose to see the disability because of his mind conditioning.

Next time when you look at something, just watch the talk of your mind. Observe your mind. That will help you to know yourself.

"You See Things As Who You Are and Not What They Are"

LESSON NO -4

Many times we fail to create leaders by keeping them safe and not giving them challenges. All organisations will have leaders who will call their team and sell their dream. Sometimes the team will mock them for the same as they don't believe in executing them. But that is the most important part of life. How it helps an individual would be evident from a scene. When there was a sudden attack by the thugs (pindaris) at night, the pindaris stormed into the hall where women were kept safe, there Kumaravarma (Subburaj) was living the life of a coward, ran and hid himself amongst the women. He was given a pep talk and challenge by Bahubali.

Baahubali beautifully delivered a quick pep talk and handed over the knife to Kumara Varma.

The one who gives breath is God.

The one who helps to sustain your breath is the doctor

The one who protects breath is a warrior.

Life gives an opportunity for every coward to become a hero. Baahubali gave that chance to him.

This motivational speech is very important, but more important than that is the motivational decision.

> **It is not sounding confident.**
>
> **It is about being confident.**

In nature, you will find the eagle will keep feeding its baby eaglet like a manager, helping his team members to be successful. Sometimes they may overprotect their team members even after growing in the organisation.

The eagle will take its baby to the top of a mountain, give a lovely glance, and offer a gentle push from the top of the cliff. The baby cries for this act of betrayal. While falling down, it develops courage and flies high. If this is not done, it will always take refuge of the Adult and will not learn to fly.

If you are a superb leader, then create leaders.

How do you do it?

Give them more challenges.

Ask them to face challenges.

Like how a caterpillar struggles to become a butterfly, allow him to develop strength out of struggle. Many of you holding this book would have been pushed into the water by surprise to learn swimming.

A good leader will offer a good challenge to their team.

If you are a good leader, do it. Push them to a big challenge and tell them that they can do it.

Baahubali gave him a good challenge and made him a great hero forever.

LESSON NO - 5

The one scene where we get goosebumps. We feel gratified for investing our money and time in watching the movie. The scene where you see Baahubali crowned as a chief commander of the Army. That shows the intensity of leadership.

John Maxwell talks about level 5 leadership.

What is such Leadership?

I respect him because

He is my boss - Title respect (level 1)

He is more talented - Ability respect (level 2)

He helps me - Utility respect (level 3)

I get my job done - reliability respect (level 4)

More than that, as a character, I love my leader. I will walk out to the war field for him (level 5).

They will be ready to give their life for the character.

In all centuries, we had people of that sort. The reason is evident - Baahubali is a kind of warrior who will get down and fight. You can see his counterpart, Bala, will sit in a chariot and fight. Baahubali will get down to action with the team.

Swami Vivekananda, in his conversation with General Strong, was amazed at the fact that the British soldiers with arms and ammunition failed in front of the Indian soldiers. Simply, a commander should go forward and offer his life first, but the British commanders went back and shouted "boys, move forward." This made the revolt of 1857.

In the film 'Billa 2', Ajith will deliver a beautiful dialogue.

"The one who sits and asks for a job and the one who gets down to action will have a huge difference."

During a Crisis, You Get Down and Control the Crisis.

Don't let the crisis control you

You need to get inside the track to get the job done. Fight with them and work with them, not just boss over from behind. Be a frontline warrior in your workspace.

Whether it is Napoleon or Alexander, they fought from the front end.

During a Crisis, You Get Down and Control the Crisis.

Don't let the crisis control you

"They Will Not Only Live for You"
They Will Even Die for You."

LESSON NO -6

In an organisation, when you have an issue, they will refer back to the protocol and HR policies.

Try to interpret the words for decision-making. With so many escalations, then so many hierarchies, they will conduct a root cause analysis. Much time will be wasted following a lot of procedures, systems, and processes that must be adhered to. Hence, we will continue following the processes, which will take more time even though we know what needs to be done to fix the issue.

When Devasena was questioned and examined in a typical corporate way, due to the political influence, they wanted to discuss the problem from a standpoint of political supremacy and not as per Dharma. Baahubali enters with force and takes swift action.

For molesting a woman, he chops off his head. He works on his principles and not on the protocol.

This is what we call.

"Work on Principles, Not on Procedure"

Louis Gerstner had written a book called 'Who Says Elephants Cannot Dance'. Though he was not from a typical software background and knew very little about mainframes, he made fast decisions to revamp IBM. People tried to stop him using the phrase "as per procedure." He would go ahead saying

Work on Principles, Not on Procedures

If your value systems are clear, decision-making will be clear. So always have a clear value system and ask the purpose for which you are doing it. For any challenge, see the principle.

In Sanskrit, there is a word called *bhavadhara* which can be inadequately translated into attitude or the intention behind an action. It is not the action but the intention behind it that matters. Bahubali never sought to show supremacy but to impart a lesson for the perpetrators of crime against women. If your intention is clear and strong, then taking action is easy.

Even Baahubali takes all action based on the dharma taught to him. He stood against Sivagami due to the principle of dharma. We all knew how much he adored Mother Sivagami.

Always know the purpose

Purpose forms the principles.

Then work on principles.

Swami Vivekananda described Sri Ramakrishna as "principles not just personality." He also advocates in his Advita philosophy that we must be principles not just personalities. Look at all heroes; they were principles not personalities.

LESSON : 7

Anushka would aspire to launch 3 arrows in a single pull. She had the intention without knowledge. The same day, during the emergency attack, Bahubali taught her how to launch 3 arrows in a single pull. All you need in life is your intention and a genuine attempt to pursue your goal. As Rumi said, "What you seek is seeking you." Just keep moving towards your goal; you will find the goal moving towards you. Act on the thought which kindles you; it is from this universe, from cosmic consciousness. Don't neglect the aspiring thought; go for it even without complete knowledge. You will find the path; it will blossom as we move forward. Imagine the day when Thiruvalluvar thought of creating the Thirukural. He had no clue about the impact the book could create; he would not have had the number of kural or the nature of each kural or subtopics, format for each kural. He acted on the thought; it's the universe that made him act with the thought from cosmic consciousness. Such great thoughts must be acted upon, not just for us but as a service to all mankind. Had he not acted on the thought, we would have missed the greatest wisdom called Thirukural. When some amazing big thoughts strike you, just act. Don't hesitate.

CHAPTER - II
LEADERSHIP LESSON FROM STAR VIJAY CHANNEL

Imagine a market where you have a super-giant dominating the media and visibility through a monopoly. They were also backed by political parties. Their programmes have had a strong regional presence for years and are very powerful at this juncture when SUN TV was well established. Vijay TV wanted to enter the game of the small screen or silver screen.

Here are the lessons: Quality over Quantity.

Quality over quantity, Swami Vivekananda says. "A group of quality people can do more in a year than a mob in a century." Quantity means nothing to me. Quality is everything. Vijay TV has followed it. During the day, we had 2-3 programmes with good quality in team, technicians, content, and delivery. They could have tied up with many agencies and signed up for more mega serials. But they chose to remain calm and asked teleshopping to do the job of fillers. They were not seduced by the number game. Having gotten a television licence, they could have chosen to make more money per hour to compete with other channels in terms of revenue. Their goal was to build a business that would stay stable and grow steadily, not to make quick money. They live up to deliver quality programmes. They had the patience to grow organically in the way they wanted to grow. It was tough for a potential player to play low and understand the market first and define their business model.

EMPLOYEES FIRST

"Customers come second" - Vineeth Nayar of HCL Technologies.

The above mantra that created evolution in HCL Technologies. Richard Branson of the Virgin Group also says, "Clients do not come first, Employees come first. If you take care of your employees, then they will take care of your clients."

Vijay TV not only took care of its people, but they celebrated them and also those who thrived well in the silver screen got elevated as mega movie stars. They created bus back banners, posters, hoardings, and publicly visible creativities with the pictures of their employees. They crafted a star out of an aspiring young talent.

Imagine the ease of connecting with which the channel would have established instantly with the popular mega serial stars by doing serials with them. They never followed the crowd; instead, with the same mega serial stars, they made them dance and gave them a different dimension in their life.

Emotion is a very powerful tool; logic leads to a conclusion.

Emotion leads to action.

By doing a big bang marketing, they triggered the passion and participation in the programme. Though it was a replica of an existing programme on Star TV. We should learn from their ability to observe the sensitive connection and the way they regionalised it. The flavour of the state Tamil Nadu was well nurtured.

Developing and grooming talent faster than the competition:

A very popular conversation: what if my employee gets trained and leaves me?

The answer was.

What if you don't train them and they stay in your organisation?

Test the talents

- Santhanam

- Gopinath

- D.D.

- Balaji

- Shiva Karthikeyan

- Jagan

- Mahesh

Many more powerful and influential talents.

It's not the skill or ability that they train or coach.

The Culture of Obedience

The culture of humility

The culture of performance

The culture of passion

The culture of openness

They just do not hire these talents, but they verify their ability to get mould. They hire people with a learning attitude and mould them according to their requirements.

They do not believe in hiring stars.

They have a team and process to create stars.

They don't want appatucker (meaning exceptionally different and talented people). They want a simple person who can learn eagerly.

Innovation over Imitation:

They never wanted to follow the typical programmes of Sun TV and Raj TV.

Things they avoid.

- News

- Songs

- Comedy Scenes

- Movie Rating

- Political Sensation

- Interview

- Drama

Though all the above the set protocol to get a minimum guarantee for getting viewed. The data in marketing survey said the same. Safe and easy way to make business with the same crowd. They changed their client focus to a different area. The age group which will watch the movie again and again. The age at which popularity and entertainment are the priority.

They targeted a young audience, for whom they designed mega serials with many youthful components and fun in them. A real product differentiator. Getting so much new manpower is needed for the same. That too, the age category was different and difficult for a mega serial for young adults, who generally will be in school or college.

Less of left brain activity.

More of right brain activity.

They never wanted news – timely breaking news. They believed that someone else could do that job. Let me entertain.

Like Richard Branson's book was named 'Screw Business As Usual' - it simply means don't do the usual way of business, do it in a refreshing way. Let's do something fresh.

Innovation(1)

Making silver screen stars sing and dance for film songs.

Innovation(2)

Make a dedicated team to create a spoof of movies, like 'Lollu Sabha' featuring Santhanam.

Innovation(3)

Sizzling the personal side of political celebrities in a talk show. Coffee couch format. First to introduce candid conversation to a Tamil channel.

Innovation(4)

The core components of human emotions, such as

-    Poignancy.

- Fun and Humour.

- Aggression and Achievement.

were incorporated into the reality singing and dancing show. People love emotion and engage with emotion rather than doing it with a usual serial they aspired to do it with reality dance shows. Especially the background BGM during any elimination in competition, making the family members of contestants get emotional and present it with powerful emotional music

Innovation(5)

Properly scripted sequence in a debate and talk show. They do a good amount of editing to really make it interesting to the audience. It is the same truth but it should have gripping content and effective editing. They do four times the work of others who hunt the audience and ensure they also do not repeat. They fill their funnel with more people and select the best. They toil so much with the sequence of the flow. They select the guest in a wonderful manner. Organising the flow is important; otherwise, just fighting will make it chaotic. They beautifully organise the flow of the talk show. Decent execution by Mr. Gopinath who will stick to his limit and do the job with passion.

Innovation(6)

Choosing programmes based on iconic celebrities rather than conducting interviews like 'who is the next Prabhudeva', more live concerts, more award functions, and more events for celebrities like Kamal Hasan.

Rather than calling people for an interview, you celebrate the celebrities in a big and sustained way which ends in a mega event. Actually, by doing this, you give them visibility and also get more visibility. In this way, the cost of operation is also reduced. A really smart business proposal executed with great speed.

Innovation(7)

Quality English and other language movies are telecast in Tamil. Introduced world cinema to Tamil. Any good quality movie is replicated. They just do not see the limit in language; they will look at the quality of the product in any language. BURFI – a great movie would be in the dark if it were not shown in Tamil for the Tamil audience. The message is more important than the linguistic and cultural barrier.

Quick Decision and Execution

They did a game show where a seasoned artist called Vijay Adhiraj was asked to conduct it.

"Tell the price and get the product."

Invested time, money, and people in branding and marketing. Very quickly, they stopped it the moment they sensed that momentum is not good enough. If my client is not excited, let me stop it at all costs.

A big actor was asked to do a game show where tricky activities were conducted within one minute.

They found something missing. The actor exited, still they executed the show with their in-house talent like D.D. who was able to create a great sensation with the game show.

The decision to adjust the sail is remarkable.

> A Pessimist would complain about the wind.
>
> An optimist would expect it to change.
>
> A leader would adjust according to the sail.

There is someone who takes clear-cut decisions and then the team gives life to the leadership. It's not just success that I appreciate but decision-making at the right time. Taking decisions with courage.

Invest in the Authentic

Look at the movies they buy. What is the one word that will influence the company to buy a movie.

"Authenticity"

If the maker of the movie has created a masterpiece. Even if the commercial success is less, they go ahead and buy the movie. This has become a part of their ethics, and they do it at any cost. They respect the genuine effort of the maker.

→ Aaranya Kaandam.

→ Moodar Koodam.

→ Oonaiyum Aatukuttiyum.

→ Burma.

→ Inidhu Inidhu.

Moreover, if they buy your movie, it simply means you are authentic. They don't buy junk, however successful it might be.

Their Phoenix Attitude

To germinate

↓

Sustain in the game

↓

Scale up to heights

↓

Excel in their work

↓

Compete with the best.

↓

Going over the Top.

Without any political background or political support, they were able to create an impact which is quite prominent and looks promising for the future.

Two top Dravidian powers of politics are operating at their best abilities and clout. Still, Vijay TV dared to come out and play their passion with the utmost innovation.

Quite some time, they were very stubborn in not telecasting movies on the channel. They later understood that they needed to be adaptive and innovative. Hence, they made a decision to telecast a movie and were innovative in selecting the right one.

They never mind repeating the good one (Kumki was repeated several times). People still watched the quality movie despite the repetition.

The market made fun of repeating movies, but the real fun element is that despite it being repeated, people watched it several times. Such was the selection criteria. Also, the invested money is taken care of well. At the end of the day, the business proposition must be a part of any move. When there is an opportunity to make more money, we should make the best use of the same. Return on investment was really smart.

> An old Benz car is still a Benz car. Enjoy the ride, feel the elegance.
>
> – Spartan Senthil

They even re-telecasted some of the favourite episodes of reality shows as fun bites which acted as a hook in seconds.

Act of Balancing

They have a good 360° feedback system, and they do not just receive the feedback but work on it continuously.

First Incident

Once in an audio launch (kumki), a favourite song of a particular sect of people was sung by a popular director (Menon) which they could not cut or edit. The hero of the movie, his father and grandfather were honoured by this act. After the telecast, they would have surely sensed a theme of biased organisational function by telecasting the event. Immediately they focused on the national leader of the other sect who is likely to feel noticed. The Sunday morning talk show was done to eulogise another leader of the sect which is totally different and by which they were able to balance this function and modus operandi. Most importantly in business, we want all clients of all sections of society. We need to prove our neutrality. In race, caste, language, nationality, culture, and religion be neutral. You require intelligence that unknowingly things happen but you should prove your neutrality.

Second Incident

When a show called Big Boss was introduced by them and taken forward, it went from good to great by collaborating with a suitable anchor.

The feedback was on the Illuminati and other 'Anti-Tamil culture kind of programme' was put forth by a group of people who were keen on pulling down the fame of Big Boss.

Vijay TV positively responded by including a lot of Tamil in the conversation. Tamil Kadavul Vaalzhthu, a Tamil writer, was asked to be a part of the crew. They came with a serial programme on the God who is very popular among the Tamil-speaking community across the world, insisting on Tamil in that programme. Furthermore, they quickly decided to launch a programme on Lord Muruga. Look at the way they named it. It could be Murugan vilayadal, Murugan Avadhaaram, Murugan Perumai, Kandan Perumai... and so on, but the strategic move was to name it as Tamil kadavulmurugan.

'Tamil Kadavul Murugan'

The name could be anything, but they were very keen to include 'Tamil Kadavul Murugan'. They ensured that this brand image is always high. They always do things to build a positive image in a more balanced way. Their smart act of executing it fast and speed of decision-making was really remarkable. They also kept flashing the advertisement of 'Tamil Kadavul Murugan' in between Big Boss.

This is because they had a solid belief in themselves and wanted to build a brand that is more balanced in approach.

> Things can go wrong, but we can always make it right.
>
> – Spartan Senthil

CHAPTER - III
STEPHEN COVEY'S PHILOSOPHY IN DHANUSH

Circle of Influence and Circle of Concern: From the life of Mr. Danush

Let me tell you about actor Dhanush. If we refer to him as an actor, few may believe, few may not believe. The reason was very simple, very obvious - his slim physical appearance. Once Dhanush was asked a question, "What is your speciality, what makes you special?" very quickly he answered, "I don't have anything special. That is my speciality." It might be a very humble statement, but he is a master. The truth is just the opposite. He mastered himself not just because of his ability to act, his ability to sing, his ability to write lyrics, and other abilities now groomed to the level of Director. But he is a classic example of the circle of influence. A classic example of "how to use your circle of influence?"

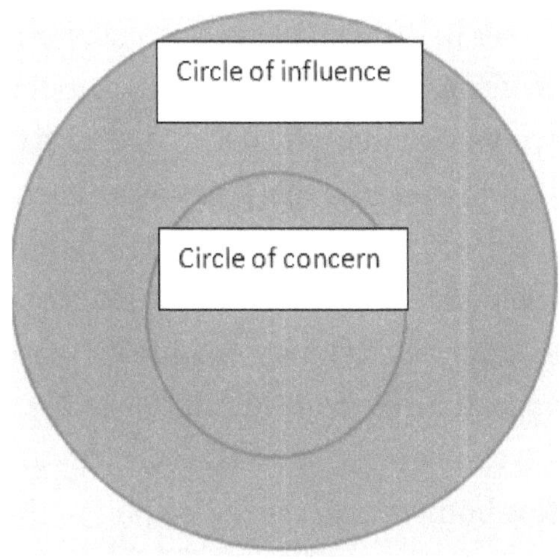

Every human being has their own circle of influence and circle of concern. The circle of influence is nothing but things that are under our control. A circle of concern is nothing but things which are not under our control. It's quite common and natural that most of us are worried about things which are not under our control and the effects they carry in our life. But few understand themselves well. They understand their potential. They acknowledge what is not with them and don't cry about it. Rather, they put all their energy into creating what is possible. They push their limits in the area of strength, not in the area of weakness. They give their best. They give everything that they possess and they try their maximum limit that they can do and they passionately do it every time. They don't bother about what is not with them. Surprisingly, what you focus on grows in life. Earlier it was tough for many of us to acknowledge him as an actor or hero. But with his physical profile, he entertained the crowd. He was able to make a difference. His self-love was so great, which opened an opportunity for him. He kept winning the game. He kept moving forward not just locally but the entire nation started knowing him. He got one of the best opportunities that he could ever get. It's not overnight. It can never be luck. He toiled day and night for this. Not bothered about the rumours, the trolls, the negative statements. He proved everyone wrong. He proved that this world is for heroes, who have the guts to do what they want to do. Eventually, his circle of influence became so big and the circle of concern became very small. He not only helped himself, he helped many people to grow in this industry. Amazing to see this. It's a real inspiration for anyone. Don't feel bad about what is not with you and feel great about what you have. Use 100% of what you have. When you use 100%, you will be blessed with more and more and more. This is how a winner is made. Truly magical let's all learn how to expand our circle of influence and acknowledge our circle of concern. Kindly write the list of things that you have and ensure within this year you use everything 100%. The negative statements were proved wrong.

People said, "Where can he go at most?"

Now he had gone for the maximum. Ha ha.

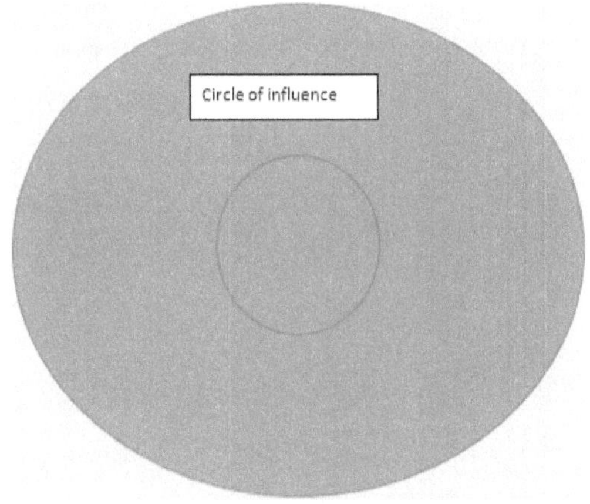

He not only helped himself, he helped too many people to grow in this industry. Amazing to see the inspiration. The message is simple - don't feel bad about what is not with you and always feel great about what you have and use one hundred percent of what you have. When you use it one hundred percent, you'll be blessed with more and more.

Let us learn how to expand our circle of influence and acknowledge our circle of concern. Kindly write a list of things that you have. Use everything hundred percent with love and passion. Contribute with all your capacity. Nature gives you an opportunity, if you don't use it well then nature will wait until you finish using it. That is why winners keep winning. What you focus on in your life grows. Focus on what you have. You will have more to focus on in the future. The way to climb 1000 feet is to take one step at a time. Keep moving, use your 100 percent.

CHAPTER - IV
THE FLOW CONCEPT - ILLAIYARAJA

Let me start with positive psychology. It is an academic psychology backed up by research. Seligman is the father of positive psychology. He worked in

- Happiness

- Character

- Concentration

The one person who worked exclusively in concentration is 'Mihaly Csikszentmihalyi'.

Eastern European origin. Worked in concentration for 30 years. He talks on a topic 'FLOW'. Flow is not a pep talk concept; it is a scientific study of concentration. Flow is scientific clinical psychology. Unknowingly, we say "I did this in a flow, I spoke in a flow" but this flow is different.

Quality of our life depends on the quality of our experience. Quality of experience depends on concentration.

In his book Creativity: Flow and the Psychology of Invention and Discovery.

You are in an ecstatic state to such a point that you feel as though you almost don't exist. I have experienced this time and again. My hand seems devoid of myself, and I have nothing to do with what is happening. I just sit there watching it in a state of awe and wonderment. And (the music) just flows out of itself.

In any work, be it music, sport, or computing, when you are an amateur, your skill will be less, the challenge will be more, and it will be frustrating as you fail frequently. Sometime later, you will eventually master the skill, where the skill will be more, the challenge will be less, and it becomes boring as you win effortlessly. At that stage of peak skill and peak challenge, you will enjoy your work without realising yourself, without the feel of 'I', and there will be a flow without your perception. It means you are operating in flow.

Enid Blyton had a flow of words and saw the characters talking to each other as she wrote. She was able to write more than 50,000 words at a stretch within a day.

The great mathematician Ramanujan wrote many equations out of his superconscious emotions pouring out through his mind. This simply means he must have been in a state of flow. You can find the supernatural feel of excellence in his music because of his ability to let it flow.

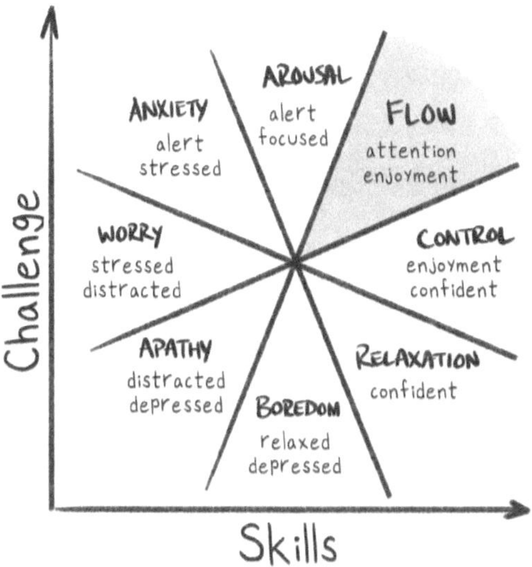

When the skills and challenges are at a certain level, you go to a state where excellence in the job comes without human effort. They called it Ayam Bhramaasmi, which states that excellence is God (Ayam means God).

Some of his compositions are just amazing; those who listen get mesmerised by the impact. The impact is truly great that he proclaims. Even he did not decipher the source of its origin.

Whenever you do something as a perfect instrument by detaching yourself from the result and totally throwing yourself into the project with absolute unselfish passion, the result will be so great that you could not imagine.

The state of flow is attained by challenging your skill, challenging yourself, and the best of your own version will emerge.

Do your work disinterested, not uninterested.

This is the essence of karma yoga and an extract from the Bhagavad Gita. I often get this question – these spiritual gurus tell us to work with interest without interest, quite confusing this philosophy. Not interested in the end result, greatly interested in executing the process of creation. Not passionate about the success at the end, total passion in just creating a masterpiece – Sarvapriyananda.

Do the work with detachment from the result and the pride of the achievement. At the same time, do it with love for love's sake. Do it with the love of just doing it.

In the 1970s and 1980s, Ilayaraja composed music for the purpose of love, not for the award or money, but to feel the vibration of the soul. Without the ego, he allows the divinity to flow, challenging himself at a great level of concentration. The Maestro's Magic with Thiruvasagam was simply inexplicable. Surely, all compositions came from the extremely calm state of mind which they call Alpha or Theta. The Alpha state of mind is nothing but a sort of meditation. His music was the outcome of meditation. Even those who listen to the music go to the same state of Alpha by concentrating on the FLOW. In the Alpha state, your breath becomes serene, and you will breathe less in number but deep in quality, probably eight complete breaths in a minute or even less. Since the mind is in an intense state, not in a tense state.

If the vibration of your brainwave is fast, it is an unstable mind.

(You are working out of desperation.)

If the vibration of your brainwave is slow, it is a sluggish mind.

(You are working out of compulsion.)

If the vibration of your brainwave is intense, it is a stable mind.

(The flow is working on you).

This intense state can be achieved while working.

It requires regular practice and constant challenge to reach flow. If the challenge is less, flow is not achieved. If ability (competency level) is less, again not possible. Only when both meet at a particular level do you reach flow. You work at a super conscious level. There is a difference between you pulling something and something blossoming through you.

Some artists, doctors, engineers, and scientists had such brilliance flowing through them effortlessly.

It involves extreme concentration and great surrender to your job (they truly feel that their job is bigger than their image). Thereby, you enjoy the concentration and eventually concentrate on the enjoyment. The end result is an intense feeling. These works are ever fresh and alive and feel updated every moment. Keep challenging yourself, reach the alpha state of your brain not by alcohol or cocaine but through losing yourself. Create great work and crush your pride and ego. You will become a Maestro. That is how you find your calling.

Remember, you are not doing a job, but you are flowing towards your calling to the earth. In short, you find yourself by losing the SELF. Your purpose becomes bigger than YOU. Creativity blossoms when you fall in unconditional love with your work!

"If you have zero-ness in you, you can see the hero-ness of your Ishtadevata in you"

– Swami Vivekananda

CHAPTER – V
SHANKAR BEYOND SIX SIGMA

Two powerful messages from Shankar

Vision and Focus

- Define his vision more clearly. "What do I want?"

- Focused on getting it done by his team "No compromise"

The project head in movie making is the director. Opinions and views could be optimised. We get opinions and suggestions from different people, to show our consideration. It is human nature to say yes and try to get inside their good books. The best boss is someone who tries to get the best out of you. He takes your evolution forward in your profession. The greatest wisdom is to be aware that if your boss is showing that he is unhappy with you because he is concerned about making you a better person in your domain. I would like to quote two incidents from the life of Michelangelo: whenever he paints a picture or completes a sculpture, he asks his father to look at the work. The first word that comes from his father is his shortcomings. However, Michelangelo had toiled with precision to create a fabulous work, but his father was able to identify the mistakes that made him excel in his work. It is quite popular that good comments and accolades are giving the energy to grow.

The one who appreciates you is like your father. But the one who points out your mistakes to your face with noble intentions to improve your work is your true godfather – Spartan Senthil.

Shankar had been a godfather to many in many ways, getting the best out of them and eventually extracting their best. Working with Shankar, everyone evolves, including him. His words are going to shape your future. Appreciation makes you grow, but critics make you evolve.

Every movie of Shankar had a vision. The surprise is he was able to look at it clearly. Every micron was clear, the execution was set in such a way that his team delivers it without any deviation from the clear vision. In this process, there were chances where some legends who are a part of his works try to create something new and special. He has the ability to accept it as special and great; moreover, his greatness lies in saying no to such a special work if it deviates from his vision (even by a micron).

You give him a beautiful set; he will accept its greatness, but if it is not seen in his vision, he says NO.

You give him an interesting design of dress and fabric; if it is not seen in his vision, he says NO. "There is power in No."

It is not arrogance but commitment to do justice to his vision. It is nothing but belief in his faith, having faith in his belief.

Again, the history of the world is nothing but the history of a few individuals who had faith in themselves.

– Swami Vivekananda

The brilliant words

Lil Wayne said, "Surround yourself with love, not friends."

Marilyn Monroe said, "I live to succeed, not to please you or anyone else."

The second incident is also from Michelangelo. He was sculpting the eyes of a baby which remains at a greater altitude in a big statue. Someone rushes out to his workplace and shouts that Michael is blessed with a child. "Okay, Thanks! I will finish all my work and come there to see my child" was the answer.

This shows his commitment. When he got down from the statue, the other person asked him, "Who is going to find out the quality of the eyes of the baby which is at an elevation above their head by looking at the artwork they will appreciate you? Moreover, it is not easily visible from the ground level. The observer can visualise it only from the view, so why do you waste your time in doing it right with so much precision."

Michael Angelo replied, "No one can find out, but I know it. How can I create something with imperfection? My conscience will not allow me to do something less than excellent."

"The key is – I know it."

That *knowing* what Michelangelo talks about is not an approximate vague picture. Inside his vision, he was certain about every nuance of what he was going to create. This clarity in vision is success. I always say that vision is nothing but the ability to see the invisible, which is yet to be formed in the world.

Vision is the capacity to see the invisible.

– Spartan Senthil

Likewise, Shankar is committed to wowing his client in the way he wants to. Since he is certain and clear about his project. Clarity is what you want and not trying to please people. Some directors feel that they should say yes to the first tune and first lyrics since it comes from a genius.

In Mudhalvan movie, the final song was almost finalised with a beautiful melody. Vairamuthu had penned the lyrics, and Rahman composed the music for it. Shankar spoke to his inner voice, which rebuked him for deviating from his faith. He had the guts to say no and demanded something else from Vairamuthu and Rahman - a fast folk number 'Uppu Karuvaadu' was born. For your information, it became a great hit. When you are in charge of the project, be concerned about the project. Do not worry about 'what they will feel'. Ask for what you want from the team.

"This is approximately close to my vision, okay! Let me take it. It is not his habit. I want it that way. It is not 99% or 101% of my vision. I want 100% of what I want; even the six sigma level is also not suitable."

So surprising that he looks at his technician's communication of the work, says No! No! No! Yet believes that this person is going to give my vision. Not losing hope in the technician, persistent in taking the project pressure to focus until the expected and exact result is obtained.

The message to young managers in corporate and organisations is to understand this perseverance and make the team and boss work in such a way that the focus is on the project being 100% correct.

"Anyone can lead when the plan is the best, lead when the plan falls apart" - Robin Sharma

The art lies in mutually agreeing to work with the code of vision. Whenever there is a grey area, they must look into the code of vision. The head must communicate that it is not my way or your way; it is the path of the vision.

Shankar says to Vairamuthu, "It's not my requirement; it is the demand of the project."

The dialogue from the Hollywood movie about basketball where the duel between players goes on leading to an ego clash within the team. Finally, the hero says, "It's not about you or me but about the team."

What is vision?

Ability to see the invisible. If you have the ability to see the invisible, you can achieve the impossible.

A classic example of pursuing your vision.

In the movie 'Enthiran', a real Mercedes-Benz was used for a fight sequence, and how the damaged Mercedes would look was shown. It was a tough task for Shankar to convince the production team. When the question was asked, "Why not use the duplicate car to reduce the cost?" his intransigence paid off. So he stuck to his decision to work with the authentic car. With the real Mercedes, I can write this with a pen and paper. Very easy for me, but human nature is to please the stakeholders. Look at the grit when he made a decision, especially on his dream project which had been his dream for more than a decade.

"What will they think of me if I insist on shooting with an original car? Will they not tag me as someone who spends money for an unwanted reason?"

He understands that every rupee spent on something that is not close to his vision is an unwanted expense. Every crore spent on something that is aligned with his vision is an investment.

This visual on screen is going to add value to my client. It is going to make them wow. That is relevant to my project, so let me not feel guilty for hundreds of voices around that say "Unwanted! Luxurious! Nonchalant director". Rather than pacifying these voices, I choose to listen to the sound of my soul and stick to my faith. The ability to stay connected to the vision and not the noises outside made him a visionary.

"A professional is just an amateur who didn't get distracted"

– Robin Sharma

This statement may create some bitterness among colleagues.

Again, a gentle reminder!

"I live to succeed, not to please you or anyone else."

– Marilyn Monroe

I can't fortify this journey in this subject without mentioning the life incident of Dr. A.P.J. ABDUL KALAM. In Wings of Fire, he has explained that on becoming the project head, he was professionally well-connected to the project and about two incidents. This will tell us about his commitment to his profession.

The first incident is a strange one where he was invited for lunch and other personal celebrations by some scientists who were his peers and friends. Until the previous month when he was a friend in the same designation, he had spent time with them. However, he then made a concerted decision to desist from visiting them, even though he knows they will feel bad. He decides to remain neutral to do justice to his position.

Absolute neutrality commands more influence on your team. When you are the project lead, stay away, stay alone, and this is not easy. It takes you closer to the vision of the project.

The second incident where a scientist approaches him for permission in the evening to take his children out to the science exhibition. Kalam gave a green signal to leave early. Unknowingly, the scientist got captivated by the work and kept working there until late at night. He felt guilty for not using the permission he got from his leader, at the same time worried about his wife's reaction to cheating the kids. The surprise was that as he entered home, his wife asked him to get ready for dinner without asking anything, and the kids were also happy. Then he found out that Kalam sir had sent a car and took the kids to the science exhibition and also accompanied them. Kalam sir did not want to disturb him, at the same time, if he needed to take the kids so that his project scientist is getting on with his vision for the day, and he helped him. Here also people may call it partiality and subject to criticism. But it is close to the vision. Do what it takes for the work to progress faster, whatever it may be.

Both the incidents have a different way of execution, but his principle is to stay true to his vision to complete the project on time.

"Run your own race, who cares what others are doing? The only question that matters is - Am I progressing?"

– Robin Sharma

He surrounded himself with love, not friends. His commitment to his vision and job is at the top of the priority list.

Be clear in what you want to do at every stage. Do what it takes to live your vision. Any confusion at any stage with anyone, listen to the sound of your vision, then go by it.

Clear vision - keep seeing, breathing, and living your vision!

Getting monomaniacally focused on your vision will give life to your project. Just look at market leaders; they are leaders because they were ready to say 'NO' to other businesses, never wanting to open restaurants or real estate projects. They just focused their energies on making their business great.

The traditional South Indian restaurant like the hotel Saravana Bhavan does what they are good at. They don't sell mobiles or cars; it is not a question of financial support or strength to focus on your craft and do it the way you want it.

They have streamlined their process so greatly that when you order 18 idlis from any part of the world, the quality remains the same. The taste will tell you the tale of titans in idly making. Just because pizzas and burgers are in, you should not grab the opportunity to diversify and deter the quality of your vision.

Steve Jobs also emphasises that focus and concentration are the key to success. When you further probe him about his view on focus, he elucidates the following: Focus is not only what you want to do or what you like to do; it is all about saying NO to anything other than what you want to create. That extreme selective nature and uncompromised vision is focus. It is not about good or bad; it is all about whether it suits my project or not. It is so binary that it is either zero or one. Have the courage to live your project.

Do everything to create a project that you exactly had in your mind, the one you saw in between your eyes.

When he took over Apple Inc., he said no to so many other products like printers and more. Let us be clear and specific on what the message is. Shankar has so much knowledge, but when he works on one subject, he will never try to interlink many issues. For example, for the social message, he will stick to it clearly.

Someone so close to your heart has spent 1000 hours to create something assuming that it will cater to your project. Have the guts to say no, "It is phenomenal, but I cannot collaborate with it." That stubborn decision in your specification will create the real you. It is not just work that you do or create. It is your vision which is there in every micron of your project. Let it be true.

Your workplace and profession are not a party hall where you need to hit maximum glasses and cheer for networking. It is the sound of your soul. Don't bury that in order to please the cacophony outside. Always remember that life begins when the chicken breaks the egg from inside; if broken from the outside, it ends. When you look in the mirror and feel that the nose could be sharper, the eyes could be more pleasant, the complexion should be better, there are surgeons who can do that to your face. But it is not your true face. You have done something that demands some sort of appeal by a large opinion, a buy-in by a large probability.

"An unattractive truth is far superior to attractive lies."

Be true to your vision. All through human evolution, the best of the best are those who manifest the greatness inside. Be true and be a legend; create your footprint.

The toughest thing in life is not just to win in any game, but to select which game to play and then put your heart and soul inside the game to get the best out of it. Not participating, practicing, or experiencing other games; this is called discipline. It is very human that people get distracted in the name of fun, entertainment, and infatuation. Their versatile aspirations suck their super divine power, creating nothing special in their world. Wanting to be a sportsman, musician, businessman, actor, speaker, or singer; this list becomes a temporary one, yet you want more. Understand what is inside and just say no to others; the world would be grateful for your work for a thousand years to come. Like we are grateful for Edison and Einstein.

"Take up one idea, make that your life, and let every part of your mind, body, and soul act on it. That is the way to success."

– Swami Vivekananda

Being what you already are, do that, not trying to do something you are infatuated with. Don't ask others for your vision; you should unlock yourself to see the vision. True vision is seen in between the eyes, not just with the eyes.

Accountability

We have witnessed that he thinks big, dreams big, and goes for a big way of living. A true testimony of the law of attraction in his life. He made people happy by contributing in an interesting way and inspired the audience to support in the form of buying tickets for his movies. There were instances where he paid a hefty amount as a producer to an Indian actress who danced for one song in his movie Mudhalvan, which surprised her, and she even refused to take the money, which was inordinate. This was done even before buying a Rolls Royce in his life. He knows how to value talents. In this defensive world of cost-cutting, he truly believed that the best way of getting more is by giving more. Not just as money but creating movie worth for the cost given by the audience. He spends money, but he gets the most sophisticated mechanism for accounting the job. He loves to employ the best-in-class professionals to get the accounting job done. He takes care of every penny spent. Let it be spent by the producer, but he ensures that it is measured and spent in the right manner in required places.

"Anything measured is always controlled." - Peter Drucker

He first drives a system, then the system will drive him. The process of governing the system and ensuring the process is carried out with full perfection so that he can focus on his job.

Man of Self-esteem not Ego!

The most common mistake made by people in life is being egoistic and calling it self-esteem. How can you differentiate that? It's very simple.

A person with ego looks at anything comparing their ability and creativity. There will be a sense of attachment even when looking at others' work. Thus, they cannot wholeheartedly enjoy the beauty of others' work. Since it is done by another human, they cannot see anything other than their prominence.

If you have a doubt whether Shankar has an ego, I have a clear-cut explanation. Not just psychological. It is very logical.

Just look at the remake of three Idiots in Tamil called Nanban. We know the creative quotient of Shankar. He just regionalised the subject matter in Tamil, regionalised costumes and crafted words suitable for Tamil Nadu. He was brilliant and extremely obedient in remaking it in Tamil with an attitude of letting it go the same way. Let me not disturb anything trying to prove my point. It is so wonderful.

I just loved it. I fell for the essence and presentation of the Hindi movie. Let it pass through me; let me be a good instrument in making my Tamil people enjoy it with a hero who is connected to this region.

The discipline to stay away from the temptation of changing something in the name of improvisation is not easy, especially for a creator like him whose imaginations are magical. How can he keep quiet in that arena?

He is a man with self-esteem and not ego.

His excellence is unique; hence, he did not want to make many significant changes since he does not want to compete with anyone.

A unique creator will not compete with anyone; he will appreciate the work as a true fan. Yes, Shankar behaved like a true fan in creating this masterpiece in Tamil.

Don't compete, make it complete.

No one is inferior, no one is superior.

We are all unique - Osho.

Shankar is an embodiment of the above statement, which was evident from his movie making philosophy.

Jack Ma in Movie Graphics and Technology

When it comes to authentic movie graphics using computer, his level of authenticity was inspiring. Why should I call him the CEO of Alibaba.com? He said

'Don't try to be the best, be the first' - Jack Ma

Lots of people will have an idea or thought to do something, but they keep delaying in executing the same since they wait for the best time and opportunity to execute it. They may have clear knowledge but will keep fine-tuning before executing the same.

When it comes to computer graphics, he was the first in this industry to use it more extensively, and the impact made people literally go crazy. Looking at the CG in the movie Mudhalvan was a treat. The movie Jeans was also a treat. If there is any technology, he was the first person to embrace it. The way he handles the camera and many other latest technologies were used by him. He was the first to invest in it. He dares to go ahead to get updated with the technology. His hunger for new things is very high. He is so eager to do something new.

In business, there is a bell curve of evolution. Let us look at the evolution in freezing things. Initially, they cut ice cubes and send them down the hill to use for freezing. Later, they placed them in a box and sold them. They had factories to make ice cubes and sell them. The evolution had a mega breakthrough when the refrigerator was introduced. If you can think of the refrigerator when people were cutting ice cubes from high altitudes, that is nothing but jumping the bell curve. If you can act on it, then you will get the advantage of being the first, since the experience you provide will be refreshing for the customers, and they will go crazy for the new cult.

Be the first to take advantage of jumping the bell curve.

For instance, there is a concept called surpetition.

Let us look at the life of these three people – Dunlop/ Goodyear/Michelin.

One person died bankrupt after selling rubber.

Another made 300 crores selling tyres.

Another made 3000 crores by selling tubed tyres.

They did not compete. They played a different level of the game called 'surpetetion'. They jumped the bell curve.

If you want to be successful, be the first to jump the bell curve and do something new and wonderful.

Steve Jobs and Shankar

We all talk big about design thinking, we cannot miss out on the importance of Steve Jobs who understood the importance of feelings related to the product design.

It is not what they think or how much they understand your product but how they feel your product makes it truly magical. The most profitable business is something that makes people feel good. Feeling is money. Emotion is the power to rule this world. I remember Steve Jobs said that he wants people to look at his phone and just lick at the phone. It should look so beautiful that it will make people do the same every time they look at it.

"Design is not just a part of the product; it is the actual product."

Any movie of Shankar will not compromise on beauty in any aspect. His selection of people, places, animals, and things will all be so beautiful. All his heroes and heroines look great in his movies. Even the character Vikram, who is considered ugly in his movie 'I', looked good. How is it possible?

How he would have explained the makeup technician: "Look, guys, he should be ugly at the same time but should feel presentable." Tough to define, but he had delivered the product with such great delicacy. He ensures that the feeling people get when looking at his movie must be great.

"Feel the magic. Feeling is Money. Emotion is the Key." When you make a product, ask yourself "how it feels". Our new age thought leader Simon Sinek beautifully describes that feelings come from the inner part of the brain but logics are dealt with at the superficial cortex layer of your brain. In his book – Start with Why?, when you name a product, just tell and feel how it sounds.

Hard Work

Do you know the kind of effort he takes to show 15 seconds of a shot in a song? He travels miles. To find that spot, he will search for a few thousand miles. Yes, what you see as locations in his movies are the end results of more locations which they see. They have a funnel to feed with fifty locations, then they crystallise it to 5, out of which one is selected. Why should he travel to forty-nine other locations? To ensure that he gives the most suitable place on the screen.

Look at the respect he has for his clients.

There are no shortcuts; he wants to ensure that they travel the distance for that particular moment. He feels that serving the best or giving the best to the best of his knowledge is the only way to satisfy the expectations of his audience. He is ready to work hard to find the best locations. For 15 seconds in a song, why harass people and himself by going to fifty locations? It is diligence and intelligence working hand in hand.

Hard work pays

Stay hungry! Stay foolish!

So many victories,

So many varieties,

So many awards,

So many fans,

Great universal recognition - Name, Fame, Money, what not?

What about the spirit of trying something new? What about the passion to deliver world-class?

Did success go to their head?

Is it alive...? Haha... The moment I saw the fight sequence in the movie 'I' on the rooftop using the special cycle in China. All my questions vanished like dew drops after sunrays.

New location.

New instrument (Off-road cycle)

New style - over the rooftop. Height of heroism!

It is clear evidence that the will and desire to improve the performance did not die. His appetite is still the same as he had during 'Gentleman'.

Wish that I should improve and let me learn more and share more in the years to come. It's just a beginning according to him.

CHAPTER – VI
RADAN MEDIA AND HER SUCCESS

Radika Sarathkumar should be lauded not just for her popularity but for her core management principles applied and leadership qualities exhibited with courage.

Sustaining your brand equity in the market is not easy. The world is competitive, and clients prefer to choose the best of the best. Only quality determines your success. "Survival of the Fittest" is the way. Every hour a director is created. Every hour new talents pop up. Every hour technology takes over the silver screen. How is she able to dominate the silver screen?

We can learn not just one but many principles from her. When I was in college, we saw her serial 'Chitti'. Now my son is in school, still the connection with Radan is on. Let's see how.

Lesson No 1

Sense the change before you get lost.

Fifth discipline of Peter Senge - Change management principle:

A frog which is jumping into hot water will immediately jump out and save its life due to its sensitivity. The difference in temperature is felt suddenly. However, if the frog sits in a water pot which is gradually heated, it may not receive the stimulus to jump immediately, resulting in its death. The same frog, but with a difference in the ability to sense the change. In business, Nokia might have been ruling the market during 1999-2005, but they did not monitor the decline in interest and missed the migration of loyalty from Nokia to Sony Ericsson, then to Samsung.

In *Annamalai* serial, the initial importance was given to the mystic old man in the temple where supernatural things were emphasised, similar to *Marmadesam*. The entire context in which the story was placed had a mystic mood. The death in the temple and the way it was portrayed was different. This is where she sensed the slowdown or decrease in interest. Very quickly, she took control of the situation, changing the focus to sentiment, emotion, and thriller, the war between good and bad. She got the audience back on track, picking up the momentum.

Though it is just tough to leave it in the lurch and turn the ship to the correct directions. She did it again. Adaptation is the key; let me share the dinosaurs and cockroach theory.

Dinosaurs were very strong animals but not adaptive. Cockroaches were not as large and strong as dinosaurs, but when the earth experienced the worst of climatic stress, dinosaurs could not survive, but cockroaches adapted. It is not the strongest but the most adaptive to the change that would survive.

Queen of adaptation

In his book Lead or Bleed, our friend Mr. Rajeev Talreja says, **"Slow to hire, fast to fire."** He not only did it with the team but also the entire way the story goes. Accept that the customer is the boss. If he hates it, then have the guts to throw it off and focus on what he likes.

> "To catch fish, don't carry strawberries and ice cream but stinking worms"
>
> – Dale Carnegie

Carry what the fish likes, don't carry what you like if you want to catch fish.

LESSON #1

Respond to the customer's behaviour and change your presentation and product according to your audience. "Sense the change and adapt." Be a good cockroach and not a dinosaur. Be responsible for consumer behaviour.

LESSON #2

Innovation and Institution

The great disadvantage of watching the serial is just getting hooked with the same characters. But that is how a mega serial works. The audience gets attached to the character and the character gets attached to the storyline. So no chance to add flavour. She implemented the greatest form of innovation. She incorporated a new strategy of getting new talents, the way they mentioned in the book 'Good to Great.'

> **"First hire good talent, board good people on the bus, then decide where to go."**

She set the trend of hunting top talents like how Apple hired image consultants when they went ahead with face sensing in iPhone X. She kept onboarding talents. Created a quick new theme and flavour. Froze their entry and exit for two to three months. Then planned their exit in the story.

Here she demonstrates her win-win-win strategy.

Win for clients: Spiced up the mega serial with new fresh talents and good-looking faces, a win for clients to see new good-looking faces in the show.

Win for the fresh talents: They move out with pride carrying a badge of Radan products, which gave them the platform to exhibit their talent. They become the Alumni of Radan, which increases their market value and popularity.

Win for Radan: The future stars who are going to charge more will be available for a reasonable charge or payment. They will not demand more. Also, the value of the show goes high.

Not a win-win for Radan and newcomers but a win-win-win for the audience.

It becomes their SIIM (South Indian Institute of Megaserial) for new talents, which will give them the initial breakthrough.

Radan becomes a school of excellence. What an idea!

Hitting Without Hurting

Everyone either supports or opposes religious ceremonies. Sometimes they feel afraid to talk about that subject. They do not discuss the real and fake things. She has the courage to talk about this subject. She is crystal clear in her views, traditional yet scientific. Throughout, we can find eulogies for ancient values and religious ceremonies. She emphasises the goodness of all the rituals without hurting. She never fails to castigate the false and fake people under the name of religion and to dupe people. She also never fails to respect the true power of Bakthi. She reveres the true form of worship and its power, and the greatness of ancient Indian medicinal values.

When Swami Vivekananda was asked, "There are so many fake Swamijis and Godmen who do tricks to deceive people in the name of religion. They use religion to steal money from people. What is your take on it?"

For that, Swamiji replied, "There cannot be any fake thing without an original. You require an original to create a fake. There are originals, and I have seen many original realised souls."

> You can communicate a good message of reform, but make sure it does not hurt people. She is a master who tells the truth without hurting any sentiments.

CHAPTER - VII
A.R. REHMAN - CLASSIC LIFE LESSONS

LESSON #1

When opportunity meets preparation, that is called luck. We become tense and tend to make mistakes during some crucial opportunities and then repent. Sometimes, during crucial times, we may get tense and make blunders due to over-excitement. But in 1992, Rehman composed music for the movie Roja - a Manirathnam movie. Getting a debut, that too in a Manirathnam movie, would make an individual in his teens get tense. Several movies of Manirathnam got accolades due to the magic of the music. There could be many factors responsible for the composition. Every factor was nature's will to invoke a musical giant to this world. His calmness and cool nerves were the key. He trusted the divine power to carry the project.

The score of 'Thamizha Thamizha' became the stepping stone for a new era in film music. When life gives you a chance, put your best into it. "When you get a full toss, just shoot it out of the stadium."

LESSON #2

The marble, which was strongly certified by many experts as a useless piece of stone, was converted into a statue called David by Michelangelo - 18 ft tall, more than 300 years old, and still looking good. Even Rahman sculpted himself, where he sculpted himself despite many criticisms, "Too much of music, no words are clear." His persistence overcame resistance. Out of the total music composition, Rahman's music was just 5 to 10% of the movie in 1993. Those days, a teacher from Dindigul (a town near Madurai) called Leone anathematised Rahman, calling his songs absurd.

- Lot of English words are used

- Very hard and heavy music score

- The voice of the singers is not good

- Music overrides the voice of the song

- He will be a shooting star and not a pole star. They sold cassettes and made stage shows making fun of popular Rahman songs, stating that the old songs were good and the new songs are just noise

Anything new will have to undergo three things:

Opposition - Don't do it.

Criticism - You can't and it won't

Appreciation - I told you he would do it.

A lot of comments were openly thrown by all the media and experts stating that this form of westernised music cannot be listened to after 10 years. It is 2024, just listen to the songs of Roja, Duet, and Puthiyamugam. It will bring tears to your eyes. The saxophone in Duet will take you to a different level of existence. Dear critics, 30 years and still getting stronger. Breaking linguistic barriers, he introduced many singers from many places outside of Tamil Nadu, even outside of India. It was fresh and fantastic.

I would like to quote the guru movie dialogue: "Remember when people speak badly about you for expressing your passion, it simply means you have chosen the purpose of coming to this earth. It is not your job; it is your calling to this earth."

In 1995, by sheer power of his quality, he forced the directors who made negative comments about his music to come forward to associate with him for their projects. Especially when you are a performer, the force which encourages you will be the appreciation. Sometimes people may feel jealous about you and start pulling you down; that is where you should demonstrate the strength of character.

"Maturity is when people try to hurt you, you try to understand them and develop the courage to serve them."

LESSON #3

He was new to the industry, just started to make money and enjoying success. His music was so enthralling that not only engrossed the people but few music directors who used his tune and started minting money and popularity out of it. Not only in Tamil language, in Hindi as well. Many directors copied his music. There were also so many pirates. Imagine so many of the pirates were already wealthy, he just started to make money. So many directors earned fame whereas he just started to earn some fame.

If you are a young executive, programmer, or manager, how would you feel when someone gets promoted for stealing your work, more so when it is evident and conspired? We tend to use abusive language at least inside our minds. We tend to make a complaint to the authority. We will initiate legal action and move to court. In fact, if Rehman had gone to court and sued those music directors, he would definitely have earned money, but even at that early stage, that was not his motto. He was particular about not earning enmity.

"Work to earn money, respect, and the heart of the customer and not to earn the enmity of competitors."

Whatsoever may be the temptation, this is also a form of charity. Thank God! That you did your job so well that made others lose their faith to compete and steal yours.

He had this maturity at a very early age. When asked, "Why don't you file a case against them?" His response was – "Why should I enter the Hindi industry with grudge and enmity?" When the press asked him, "Are you not cheated?" His conviction was very clear: "As long as you know that you do God's work, who can cheat whom." He always meant that he is an instrument and God is the master who is using him as a medium in rousing his music.

LESSON #4

From the year 1997 to 2002, you can find that the predominant *Gaana* thrived well in the Tamil cinema industry. It's a form that radiated the feel of Chennai; such Gaana songs use a specific style of lyrics. Although Rahman produced good quality music, the number of movies and commercial success rate of Rahman was less compared to the Gaana numbers. Sometimes, the sales of Gaana music surpassed Rahman's music. Again, there was a gang of critics to pass comment on his commercial success. For any professional, when you see the commercial success going down, they may try to move out or stop working since the reward was slow or low.

Like the rare seagull in the book called Jonathan Livingston Seagull. There, Jonathan practised flying, putting his life at risk in pursuit of excellence. Like the founder of Sony, Akio Morita lived and loved quality, survived the Hiroshima bomb. Getting obsessed with quality, Rehman did not move out of his style of work, never wanted to do something losing his quality. His balance was so great that he never altered his style of working.

In search of excellence, endure and strive for the best. Don't deviate from your service to excellence. Dig deeper in the same place to get the fresh water you wanted. Live by your conscience and stay committed.

LESSON #5

Humility, Dignity, Divinity

Once your success keeps soaring, chances are that you tend to rest on your laurels and forget to toil that is required to achieve success.

Richard Carrion, the CEO of Puerto Rico's top bank, said, "Nothing fails like success."

Sometimes success may go to your head and hinder the mission to excellence. But Rehman is very humble to the audience and fans. Your approach is very important. The most respected writer of the modern era, Amish Tripathi, of Immortals of Meluha, said.

"When I approach the book with the humility of a witness, the book will come. If I ever approach the book as a creator, it will stop."

The more Rehman grew up, the more humble he became to his singers, technicians, directors, and other stakeholders. The more successful you and your organisation become, the more humble and devoted to customers you need to be. Like a few bamboos which, on getting tall and growing in height, tend to bend down to this mother earth. Bow down to the basics, respect the basics which offered you the foot to stand and grow.

Divinity:

A modern musician in this modern, globalised music era, this world-class person has one good habit. Yes, habits form your character. And character is everything.

"There is a voice that doesn't use words... so listen"

I could witness by and large people open their champagne either for celebration or for failure. 'Pleasure or pain, pour it on my mouth' was the modern mantra. In every workplace, irrespective of gender, people want to burst their stress using liquor. They want to rejuvenate and energise using liquor.

Thousands of examples exist where people who partied so much that the next day's performance was spoiled. I still remember terminating a solid performer who was promoted to a manager and transferred to the Nizamabad branch in Andhra. He arrived late to his induction. In front of the regional head and business head, he was out of control (hungover). It turned out to be his last day in our company. It ruined his professional life, and everything was over.

There are music directors who drink and get drunk to compose music, believing that they reach an alpha mind state using alcohol. They feel that creativity blossoms with alcohol.

But in Rahman's studio, when you enter, you will feel that God is residing inside. He will light up an incense stick; its divine fragrance will invoke divinity. This habit he inculcated from maestro Illayaraja, who also worships his profession.

Devotion to your job will make you iconic. My job is mightier than me; I am what my job has made me. We can find many people in many organisations proudly blowing the trumpet, stating I did this, I made it happen, and I'm the one responsible for the success. Everything happened because of me. I taught them, 'All credit goes to me' - was the feel. They are so innocent that they don't know that we are instruments and divinity flows through the instrument. Some great people understand that they are instruments; the moment they realise this, they start to do wonders. That surrender to the super force is a great virtue.

My work is my identity. I prostrate with devotion to my job. Nothing will distract me in arousing its sanctity. Men form habits, and habits form the future.

HIS MESSAGE AFTER THE OSCARS.

Yes, we all know *Ella pugazhum Iraivanukkae.*

'Glory to God'.

LESSON # 7

He gave a short but powerful message to mankind from his soul after receiving the Oscar award.

"All my life I was offered a choice of love and hate. I choose love and I am here."

I choose love! Let this reverberate in your ears. Put love into all, believe every human deserves love in your workplace. There are people who bully you. Who make fun of your work. Who shout at you (probably the boss). Who misunderstand you and take you to HR. "He is taking my pencil, rubber, pen and pen drive" For no reason, try to prove that "you are bad I'm better than you", they may be constantly gossiping and irritating you. They may even form a faction and circulate on WhatsApp to make fun of you.

Remember when you touch social media you have two choices.

When you enter home, you have two choices.

When you enter the office, you have two choices.

When you talk to your boss, you have two choices.

When you talk to your subordinates, you have two choices.

You have two choices.

1.   Love

2.   Hate

Please choose love and become iconic.

That too, he uses a word called unconditional love.

"UNCONDITIONAL LOVE."

Do you know the meaning of it? You love someone just because you feel the love is called unconditional love. You do not expect a word, gesture, thing, not even time from the other person. Just keep loving them and even if you do not show any sign of love to them, you do not intend to reveal the feeling you have for them. You are totally satisfied by the love that you have within; you do not want to prove a point to them about how big it is.

I still remember soon after the birth of my son, from my home in T. Nagar I travelled to Chrompet

(25 km in Chennai) to my mother-in-law's house by bus, got down, took a share auto to Hastinapuram terminus, walked down a kilometre to see him. Since the water works pipeline was in progress, I cannot use my car or even my bike, without fail every evening from 6 to 9:30 p.m. I travel. In the morning by 5:30 a.m., I should start from there again. Now the question is "Will he think of me?" More so, he was just born and does not even know that I do this. Hey buddy, not only me, but every father would also have this feeling, and this is unconditional love. If you still have a question about unconditional love, watch *Thavamaai thavam irundhu.*

This same feeling he has for music. He also has it for all of us. He showers his unconditional love on us. A lot of us also shower the same upon him.

Not expecting anything, just expressing love.

Have unconditional love for what you do. Have unconditional love in all relationships. Utter this word, close your eyes, and feel the unconditional love.

LESSON # 8

Communication :

Communication is not just words but what is the intention behind it. In Sanskrit, they call it *Bhavadhara.*

Language that you use to communicate is very important. People use English, Hindi, Telugu, or Tamil. But Rahman, though he knows many languages, his preferred language was – Respect -. The most preferred language is respect.

"It is the lion that can understand the power of the elephant, not the rat" - Swami Vivekananda.

The musicians arranged for a function in Chennai when A.R. Rahman got his Oscar award and came back to his city. Rahman refers to Raja sir (the great Ilaiyaraaja sir). Rahman had great respect for Ilaiyaraaja sir. He openly recognised the greatness of Raja sir. Annakili was the first music composition of Raja sir.

"If the ways and means by which a song could be positioned in the game of Oscar nomination were known earlier, Annakili would have won five Oscars."

Look at the acumen of respect which is seen here. Respect is not something he developed as a skill; it was his way of living.

His mother tongue is respect.

"Even when you disagree, please disagree with respect."

– Spartan Senthil

He values people; he used to respect not selectively, but as the only way to respond to his peers. Respect should be the language of communication. Every thought and word you use, 'respect' is mandatory.

Just because you get promoted, change jobs, sometimes you are in a better package than your seniors, do not underestimate that money, position, power, recognition, and awards are not special to you. Do not show pomposity to your professors, lecturers, teachers, and friends.

LESSON #9

I have a mother!

He proudly made the following explanation at a felicitation.

A simple and great message from him, it's similar to the words of Shashi Kapoor in a Hindi movie who says, "I have my mother with me". The power of gratitude, grace, happiness, loyalty, and compassion has a certain frequency of positive vibration. A mother's love is something that transcends all the positive feelings. The blessings of a mother are a feeling that invokes dormant power inside a human.

A task that is very excruciating
A challenge that is breathtaking

**A hurdle that is tough to pass
Everything Will Be Cleared by a Mother's Love.**

Her grace is sufficient where all the holiness and divinity resides. He knows achieving great things is possible since he has a mother. All the Vedas have proved that a mother's blessing is essential to become great in life. We are very busy and do not have the time to talk and think about mother, but we are her heartbeat and lifeline. We are the meaning of her prayers. All her prayers are about us.

Get the blessings of your mother and father; you are halfway there on the journey of success.

He believes the success in his life is a product of his love for his son. His blessing is sufficient. Their blessing will place you in the orbit of excellence. A man who never forgets this power cannot be beaten in any place.

LESSON #10

FROG STORY

Superstar of Tamil cinema, Rajinikanth once told a popular beautiful story.

"All the frogs gathered to scale the new tower which is very tall. Then began the competition; few gave up in the initial stage, the spectators kept shouting, 'come down you cannot do it you may die since the tower is slippery, logically not possible, do not break your legs.' Few frogs gave up after scaling a small distance. Despite all these comments, two frogs reached the top. The two frogs which reached the top were deaf frogs. They were indifferent to all negative comments.

"The less you respond to negative people, the more peaceful your life will become."

Rajinikanth appreciated Rahman as a siddha for being cool with the negative people. Easy to make the statement but tough to live the statement.

Rahman never responded to cynical people. He kept jumping high like a deaf frog. Do not respond to negative people.

LESSON #11

The second frog story was about a small frog that fell inside a vessel of milk. It tried jumping out, but all efforts were in vain since it did not possess the height to come out.

It had two options, either to lie idle and die or to keep pushing the milk and keep trying.

For hours together, it kept churning; finally, after a few hours, a thick layer of butter evolved. It made the butter a stepping stone and came out of the vessel.

Before getting Oscar, look at the subsequent 2 years of cinema music; his number of songs was less. Actually, the number of hit songs really will help you boost your morale. He kept kicking like the frog jumped up to a great height, and the ATM (Azhagiya Tamil Magan song) was not initially recognised as a hit. Its performance was very average. Sometimes people may also fail to appreciate good music; still, there was a surprise element, which later resonated as the 'Jai ho' song, becoming the Oscar anthem of the year. He kept kicking and came out as a star.

Do not ask God to make you good; he will not give it to you.

He wants you to be great.

Keep pushing and doing your job in spite of tough times; greatness will evolve.

LESSON #12

EGO and ANGER

One factor that will make you iconic is 'crush your ego and feel the greatness' which is already inside you.

To be great, sense that you have an ego. Accept it, acknowledge it, laugh at it, laugh at yourself, laugh at all the funny things that you do artificially to show off. Automatically, the ego will go. For Rehman, the quantum of ego was less. He did not carry the ego.

He was free and great. People who have a high EGO obviously have a greater quotient of anger, which they misperceive as courage. You can never see Rehman sir getting angry. According to me, anger is a symbol of impotency. Those who conclude that their future cannot be controlled by them and feel that they lack substance will only get angry. Anger is like an acid that damages the container which poses it rather than the person to whom it is thrown upon. Don't store anger in your heart and corrode the walls of creativity. Faith in yourself will make you strong.

Ego and anger should be replaced by humour and faith.

Purity, Patience, and Perseverance are the three essentials of success, and above all, Love - Swami Vivekananda

Love love love!

Just do it now!

As Subramaniya Bharathi said,

Love is the ladder of life!

You man, hence, fall in love!

Rehman sir will hardly get angry with people or things since he understands the greater purpose cannot be achieved by anger.

CHAPTER – VIII
LESSONS FROM – GLADIATORS AND PORCUPINE – TEAM WORK

One of the Great Movies in World History Could Be Gladiator.

Message for the Leaders

A typical corporate scenario - Do you know the big battle which a CEO faces, the battle faced in the heart, fought in the heart is the greatest and toughest. The internal battle is the toughest.

Just visualise the scene where the group of slaves, without protective guard and without any kind of protection, are standing in the arena to fight the kings standing in a chariot with fully protected body and face. Psychologically, it will create pain in the hearts of the slave fighters to face the warrior in the chariot.

A clear-cut message for handling situations in corporates, where the organisational expectation is high, risk is more, resources are less, external support is absent, no one is aligned with your mission, there is no team and just a group of people, survival becomes a question mark, filled with fear, no hope, everyone in a slave group wants to escape the challenge. All the heads of marketing, sales, accounts, finance, IT, HR, and operations sometimes behave like a group of slaves. Everything may be against you, you may not have any external favourable situation, still everything can be overcome by what is inside you, what comes from the deepest part of your consciousness.

As described by Shri Krishna, a warrior, statesman, coach, and genius makes his affirmation in the Bhagavad Gita: "Right thinking is the key for success, all sufferings are the result of wrong thinking."

> **All you need is your inner vibe.**
>
> **Everything will fall into place eventually.**
>
> **If the vibe is right**
>
> **Go ahead and fight**

If you can communicate that to your team, they will become the powerful steam! Your thoughts and words make the water steam.

Those are not just words; those are great mantras full of life and vigour.

Actually, you don't need resources, just make your people resourceful and build trust. Russell Crowe comes out with a supernatural profile of greatness and a unique way of handling the contest as a slave. He gives a quick message to all the fellow slaves who were surrounded by the warriors in chariots. The fight was between the warriors and the slaves standing on the ground with swords. The slaves were of a mixed white and black race, unknown to each other. With no sense of bondage or purpose of existence and wanting to be selfish. "My life is more important than the fellow slave," was running inside their minds; this may create friction among the slaves. Understanding the situation, Russell Crowe quickly gave the message.

"Whatever comes out of the gate, we will all stand together and fight. United We Survive."

Individuals who stood alone, hoping to save themselves irrespective of the fellow slaves they believed in their personal strength, got chopped by the warriors and the sword at the periphery of the chariot wheel. Despite individual good power and talent, they lost. Whereas as a group together, they synergised their inner strength, stood united with a common goal and killed all warriors in the chariot. Russell Crowe did a brilliant move by being a catalyst in creating a team out of a group. He quickly made them realise the power of working together. It is good to believe in personal strength, but it will be great if we can together help in getting the best out of everyone.

The opponent and challenge may be formidable and very powerful. If you can create a team, you can defeat any powerful individual with any amount of authority.

"A group with a common goal is a team" - principles of management.

'If your team is united, the world is at your feet'

Similarly, when you look at the porcupines, you will understand that during cold conditions where their outside temperature is very low, survival becomes very tough since the extreme cold condition may affect the basic existence of a porcupine. They must stay together since by staying together they generate heat by touching each other's bodies. Each porcupine has close to 30,000 quills which are very sharp. Few porcupines may stay together, few may be alone. During adverse situations, it is advisable to stay together and work as a team. In the principles of management, they clearly define that a group or mob doing something for commercial benefit with individual interest will not do great work, whereas a group of people who have a common goal and big picture will do wonders. This is where we need to create a team from a group of people.

By being together, they may feel uncomfortable, but they need to be together to fight the situation outside. During the Chennai flood in December 2015, a similar situation was seen.

"United we survive."

There is a general opinion that caste is bad; instead, I see that as a team. The team system hampers the harmony and growth of our country. We have a different perspective to be seen here. In Tamil Nadu, we have different castes, but I would like to quote a few people who created a positive impact using team spirit.

A group of people who lived near the Kaveripoompattinam coastal area to do business and trade through sailing built a great amount of wealth by sailing outside and travelling to places. After the destruction caused by the sea, they moved to a place called Karaikudi. They went to places like Burma, worked hard, did business in a smart way, and created a great empire. They became geniuses in accounts and handling business. They used caste to help each other and improve business.

Another group of people in Thoothukudi and Thirunelveli branded them as Annachi, focused on retail provision business where they thrived in entire Tamil Nadu. They are not just successful, but they are leaders in their area of retail provision. They get down to their business and the entire community still gives competition to giants like Walmart and Big Bazaar.

Annachi Kadai always rocks. During the 1960s, people came from villages to Chennai. They got access to a union through which they were provided with weighing balances, weights, and initial materials (without any deposit) to start a business for anyone who travelled all the way from Tirunelveli to Chennai with an aspiration to start a provision business. They were encouraged to do business and grow. They encouraged each other.

They were the Past, Present, and Future Superstars of their domain. They helped each other by setting up the business model and developing it. They have rooms and offices in all cities which help their community people to stay and attend counselling for education or interviews – People from rural places can come and stay paying less or free through their union. At least in the name of a caste or sect, a human helps another human.

The third community lives in the Kongu belt. They rule the textile market and are multimillion-dollar business people who take care of exports to different countries. They teach their kids the importance of profit and the key skills to do business. Many business tycoons are created in the Kongu belt of Tamil Nadu. They help each other. If anyone suffers a loss in their business, others will pump up the stimulus package and introduce clients for gearing up in their business. In the name of caste, they help people. Ultimately going back thousands and thousands of ages, we will all be of the same family. Still, the thumb rule is very clear.

'United we survive'

To create unity

Create Themes like

Same School

Same College

Same Country

Same Caste... Soon.

Try to unite using country, caste, region, or any other reason. Don't divide using them as a reason.

In the book called 'Seven Habits of Highly Effective People' by Stephen Covey, you can see the habit called synergy. Yes, we need to synergise with the group to excel in our business. Share your strength, create bonds using inner strength, and help each other.

'1+1=2'

But with synergy 1+1= more than two - the bonding between the two creates a magical force and result - together we can do more.

CHAPTER - IX
CHINESE BAMBOO VS VIJAY SETHUPATHI AND SIVAKARTHEKEYAN

The Bamboo Philosophy

I would like to tell you the story of a Chinese bamboo.

A man bought the seeds of the Chinese bamboo variety and having sown it in his garden for one month and regularly watering, nothing came out. In his absence, he instructed his wife to water it diligently, which she did. He watered for two years, and nothing happened. His wife and kids started to mock him for not giving up and still hoping for the bamboo tree to come out even after watering for four years. He then watered for the fifth year and went to the shopkeeper and told him that he did not get any result after watering for five long years. The shopkeeper advised him to further water it for a few more months, please.

The man endeavoured to water the plant for the next eight months.

Within eight months, the Chinese bamboo shoots up to the level of an eight-storey building, sixty to eighty feet in the next eight months. The new inmates of the neighbouring house told the man, "You are lucky; within eight months, this plant grew up to a height of eight feet, super lucky." Similarly, people look at the growth of the actor called Shiva Karthikeyan and think that he is lucky. But just compare the hours he faced the camera when he did the job of an anchor. He stayed long nights, back-to-back slogging himself in different programmes, taking up different responsibilities, and experimenting with different tasks of dancing while he was hosting. Then more hours of working with relatively less salary now ended up in a status where it is vice versa. The amount of money and success got magnified to an enormous level within a short span. Actually, the tree got watered and developed its roots during the initial five years. When the foundation became strong, it took off its vertical top growth. Similarly, the hard work, passion, and dedication he put forth during his initial days supported him in emerging as a top hero in Tamil cinema.

If you fail to water during the formative years, the bamboo may die.

If Vijay Sethupathi felt that his talent was not recognised 10 years before, he would have quit. But he knows he is doing the right thing.

If Shiva Karthikeyan fails to nurture his attitude during his initial projects as an anchor, he would have killed the hero inside.

Keep watering your attitude with hope regardless of the result or size of the project.

If the man paid attention to the crowd of trolls, like his wife who mocked him for watering, he would not have succeeded.

Similarly, if Shiva Karthikeyan stopped working, since the profile of an anchor is too small for his capacity, he would not have succeeded.

Vijay Sethupathi did many small roles and short movies, aspiring to become an actor. He took up acting courses and did exceptionally well without any reward. His dedication was exceptional without a single rupee. Many people who took him lightly then got surprised by the quality of work he did. With great respect, he did every project that came his way. If Vijay Sethupathi had felt that the small roles were too bad for his super potential and negated those, he would not have survived financially. We all would have lost watching a genius actor in our lifetime. It may test your patience, but in the process what we do is more important than what we get. Some young minds say, "My aim is something else, why should I do this?" - If this is your question, let me affirm you that the current profile or opportunity will only lead you there; you cannot directly jump into anything without starting small.

Potential becomes prominent with passionate practice.

Practice does not make you a success, but passionate practice makes you successful.

Pay attention to your practice; your current job should be done well since it helps you to evolve. Your dedication and passion in the given opportunity are more important than the opportunity.

"In spite of doing small roles, Vijay Sethupathi succeeded not because of doing the small roles, but because he did those small roles so well, he succeeded."

"Inspite of working as an anchor, Siva Karthikeyan became a hero, no, he did his job 200% without expecting to be a hero, and he succeeded."

Those periods when you initially work are nothing but growing your roots. Kindly celebrate the opportunity or symptoms of opportunity. This will fuel you to reach your success.

If you celebrate what you have, you will have more reasons to celebrate more in life.

- Sometimes success is not seen outside; we must feel it inside.

- Do your work alone and do not expect instant results.

- Don't get upset by naysayers.

- Do your job in a great way. You will do a great job.

- Celebrate the journey for success is not a destination but a journey.

Except for the plant, no one knows that it is growing deep inside the ground. Actually, we must feel the success inside, though we may not see it outside.

"Growing is natural, not growing is unnatural."

– K. K. Bajaj - Chairman, Bajaj Capital

Please understand that every day in every way you are getting better and better. Kindly understand and be grateful for the natural growth and success. For you can feel it, not just see it outside.

"Feel your success inside, so you can manifest it outside one day."

The most important thing is to feel your growth and success... every second!

CHAPTER - X
ANIRUDH MUSIC AND ABDUL KALAM MESSAGE

Anirudh Music and Abdul Kalam Sir's Message:

Why should I connect two different people in two different areas of excellence? Kalam sir cannot be compared; still, a particular trait must be understood.

Music is a great therapy. It can take you to a different level of consciousness. The Indian film music industry has witnessed many great directors in the past. In the recent past, we can find the new sensation which is taking the industry by storm. Yes, it was the music director Anirudh.

I would like to mention the Wright Brothers and Samuel Pierpont Langley, which I read about in an article.

During the year 1900, there was a person named Samuel Pierpont Langley who was involved in the project of creating aircraft.

- Goal was ambitious to create a flying machine.

- Public interest was high in developing airplanes.

- Money was readily available - surplus funding.

- Associated with government and business.

- 50,000$ funded grants.

He pulled the best minds of the world (scholars/doctorates).

- Press followed them everywhere.

- The world was waiting for his history.

For the Wright Brothers

- No Funding

- No Govt. Grants

- No high-level connections

- No one was a graduate

- Humble bicycle shop

1903 – The Wright Brothers did it. The first flight when the Wright Brothers did the flight take off.

There were people around who said, "It will not take off" when they tried to fly. The people around made a comment, "It will not fly," when they tried to land. The people around made a comment, "It will not land." When the Wright Brothers landed, they were surprised.

Similarly, there are thousands of people who move to countries to learn keyboard, programming, and music composing. They do degrees in many colleges.

Amidst all the complex things, what made Anirudh succeed was a trait that is very uncommon. Moreover, he was passionate and never dreamt of achieving this name, fame, and money at this stage of life. His intention was just to feel the fun in his unique way.

"Quality of the creation reflects the quality of the creator."

You constantly communicate with the customer not by Facebook, WhatsApp, Twitter, or through newspapers or interviews. You communicate with the customer through your product and their experience. The experience that you give them is the communication. It's not just the advertisement or a brand. A brand is a promise, the value that makes the brand promise prominent.

When I read through the autobiography of Dr. A.P.J. Abdul Kalam, lots of things inspired me. But this one word hit me so deeply, and its impact was really profound.

"Simple inside, Easy outside."

These words are extracted from the book *The Wings of Fire*. Each one of us is born with a divine fire, our efforts should be to give wings to the fire and fill this world with the goodness of its glow.

The special characteristic of Abdul Kalam, sir, was being very simple.

His dress - very simple.

His family is very simple.

His book is very simple.

His humour is very simple.

His message is very simple.

His hairstyle is very simple.

His leadership is very simple.

His body language is very simple.

His approach is very simple.

His attitude is very simple.

The core tune of Anirudh will be very simple. You will find the lyrics go well with the music and its theme. Sometimes it may even sound like school rhymes. He has the confidence to term his product as a flop song (*why this kolaveri?*) and made it a hit. Being yourself is a great bliss. Feeling yourself is another bliss.

With simple music, the kind of sounds and vibes, his superb composition will make it more attractive and presentable. A sound engineering which is class apart.

"Quality is not just about the product but also the way it is served."

Grand choice of Instruments

Make small changes

Grand sound engineering

But the core music and lyrics are very simple.

Simple

Familiar Feel

Fame

Also, we live in an era where people have access to earphones and ultra-modern speakers, where the minute details are captured and delivered. This also ensures that the customer experience is great and magical.

> People feel comfortable consuming products that they can understand. Though they may be excellent products, if they are complicated, they will not create a market.

Just make it simple, obviously it will be powerful.

Don't underestimate the power of simplicity. If you still doubt that simple people can influence. I request you to listen to the speech of Abdul Kalam, sir,

Very Indian accent

Very common words

Very powerful messages

A communicator par excellence.

His words are full of love and light. The gathering in the United Nations saluted when he spoke about Kaniyan Poonkundran's words,

Be simple and powerful. Go, rule the world with love.

To reiterate, once British Airways was running at a loss and they were looking into MIS, connectivity, manpower, operational cost, salary of the seniors, and fuel cost... much more. The problem looked complicated but the solution was simple. They removed one olive leaf from their food served, and it became a profit-making enterprise.

Similarly, in a soap manufacturing unit, out of 1000, one box came empty from the factory conveyor belt line. They were about to employ a scanner and a day-night shift person to check. Many professionals with MBAs and doctorates suggested big techniques. A foreman told them to place a high-speed fan which will knock off the empty box.

The most recent simple way to make sure vehicles move quickly at the signal is to automatically set the timer to 4 seconds and keep popping the yellow light.

Again, think simple. Problems are complicated, but solutions are simple.

Simple products are easy to Enter, Progress, Prosper.
In any market!

CHAPTER - XI
FATE FAVORS THE FEARLESS - ELON MUSK, VIKATAN, COLUMBUS, STAR WARS

"History of the world is nothing but the history of a few individuals who had faith in themselves."

– Swami Vivekananda

Can you imagine moving from Trichy city to Chennai city by riding a bicycle for more than 300 km in search of a career? Can you dare to become super rich by choosing the right thing in an ethical way?

Can you put all your earnings into a single project called Chandralekha and bet on yourself? If that movie goes for a toss, he would have become poor in his life. But for him, life is lived once at the edge of a cliff. As Osho says, he experienced risk at its peak.

In Bhagavad Gita, Krishna says, "Nothing to lose but the whole world to win."

"If you are ready to lose"

"You will always win."

I am talking about the founder of Vikatan, the so-called 'AnandhaVikatan' who dared to create his destiny and more. So, a culture of ethical aggression.

His organisation will not compromise ethics for aggression nor aggression for ethics. It thrives on both aggression and ethics.

Another young man who was interested in the internet and single-handedly worked hard and founded a company (in a rented apartment) called PayPal, then he learnt and understood the way to build a rocket.

Even rocket science is not rocket science for him. His passion for making rockets was higher than the pain of losing money. He understood that they were artificially priced high. He travelled to Russia, came back with a dream. He spent money on launching a rocket. He failed. He got more money and launched a second one. He failed again. He borrowed more money and launched, only to fail again. He borrowed even more money and launched for the third time, and once again, he failed.

He had just one day left to file for bankruptcy, and people asked him, "What are you going to do tomorrow?"

His reply was simple – "I am going to launch a rocket." You know what? He launched the fourth one and he succeeded. Millions of dollars came as investment, and he came out of bankruptcy.

He owns a company called Tesla. The gentleman is Elon Musk.

"Whenever there is a battle between head and heart, go with the heart. Even if you fail, the heart can take care of you."

– Swami Vivekananda

'Men of heart get butter, and the buttermilk is left for men of mind'

– Swami Vivekananda

I cannot control myself from writing about the decision taken by the chairman of Sony, Akio Morita.

Before the 'Walkman' was introduced, Sony did a survey to find out whether the product would be accepted by the people or not. All the survey agencies worked day and night, did a lot of surveys, and they came out with a conclusion stating that the "Walkman will be a failure." This was presented to the board. Akio Morita saw the report, understood the meaning and business implications, and kept quiet for a while.

Then he released the Walkman and proved that the survey results were wrong. He believed in his product and had the fire to keep the mission going.

I would like to present a quote by Sir Winston Churchill.

"Sure I am that this day, we are the masters of our fate, that the task which has been set before us is not above our strength and its pangs and toils are not beyond our endurance. As long as we have faith in our own cause and unconquerable will to win, victory will not be denied to us."

During ice skating, you will find that the steeper the terrain, the more you should bend forward towards the steep, not away from it, to keep going.

"Run towards the fear, and you will find that the fear will run away from you."

During the expedition, the captain called Columbus and warned that the food would be enough to go back, and we do not have hope to find the new country. "Let's retreat back to the shore to be safe and in good health," exclaimed the crew. Columbus sat back, calculated, and told him that he would starve from then on, and his portion of food could be offered to the crew, by which they could go further for another day. To tell you precisely, the next afternoon they reached America.

Mahendra Singh Dhoni gets down to bat, jumping the batting order to face Muthiah Muralitharan and Kapil Dev, scoring a world record against Zimbabwe, 175 not out. Glenn Maxwell batted with cramps on Nov 7, 2023, against Afghanistan. Kumble bowled ten overs with a fractured jaw. Sachin bled and batted in his debut against Pakistan in his teens; all show resilience against unfavourable situations.

Soichiro Honda left his school, pledged jewels of his wife, slept on the work floor day and night, created a pistol which was rejected by Honda. After two years of part-time schooling, he worked and succeeded in getting it, but it was destroyed by war bombs. He used the remnants of the bomb, but still failed. Finally, he created the Super Cub by attaching a motor to a cycle to evade the crisis. He then wrote 60,000 letters to cycle owners; few responded positively, and then he became successful.

Fate favours the brave. Kindly demonstrate bravery.

CHAPTER - XII
ATTAPATTU AND D. IMAAN

Listening to Harsha Bhogle, I got inspiration to pen down the connection between cricketer Attapattu of Sri Lanka and the great music director D. Imaan.

Marvan Attapattu played well within the country, practised very hard, got selected at many levels, and eventually, one day he got confirmed for representing the country. The big dream to dress up in the country's jersey representing the nation in cricket, full of dreams and aspiration to begin a journey, he stepped up in the international arena of cricket. During his debut in test cricket internationally for Sri Lanka, much awaited by his father, mother, friends, and well-wishers, he scored a duck in the first innings. The next time in the second innings he went on to bat but got out without a run.

They dropped him. A sad moment, but he picked himself up. So he decided to go back to the nets for more practice. He practised and performed well in the games within the country. After 1 year, he got another chance. He was very keen to create an impact but he scored a duck in the first game and a '1' in the second innings. This time it would be deep frustration, then he came back after 1 year and 5 months. He scored ducks in both innings. After this, the next chance may or may not come. He went back and got a chance after 3 long years. He started with a decent innings then scored over 5000 runs. He scored 16 centuries and two double centuries.

It took more than 5½ years to prove himself at international level. Within the country, he played well, but to get a break and take his game to the international level, he kept working hard.

D. Imaan, the great music director, sizzled with his genius material in Krishna Dhaasi (a mega serial on the small screen) in the year 2000. Just in his teens, his mettle was simply amazing. Whatever opportunity he got, he gave his best – Kolangal.

Finally, he had his breakthrough in 'Khadhale Swasam'. Wow! What a feeling for a person who lives and loves music. He aspired to entertain us through film music. It was a true blessing to get elevated to do film music during his early twenties. The music was sensational, especially the song *Machee* danced by Arvind Akash. During my engineering college, we danced to the song and eagerly waited for the movie to celebrate this music director. When the moment was right, somothing went wrong, and the movie didn't get released. Dreams, hopes, aspiration... but after that, he braved into his next project. Nobody can stop the sunrise. Yes, nobody can stop his music film debut.

2002 – Thamizhan, 2003 – Whistle, 2004 – Giri

"When the going gets tough, the tough get going."

In 2012, he had a magic called **'kumki'**. After kumki, he became the great music director. A splendid, solid stuff of excellence.

Remember from Nov 2001 till Dec 2012, his resilience was exceptional. He did everything to prove his respect and passion for music. He collaborated with a team to release an album with Namitha. He never settled for living an ordinary life. He was passionate about contributing to the world. His passion was so great and the faith was simply out of this world.

Understand that not just standing strong but staying long is the ultimate success song.

He stayed in the game, played with hope, and gave the magic to himself. Resilience is the key. Both Marvan Attapattu and D. Imaan exhibited resilience in their profession. Remember the duck in his first debut. Remember the movie Kadhalae Swasam that did not get released. I recall the words of wisdom pronounced by Dr. A.P.J. Abdul Kalam, "All order comes out of disorder." Jack Ma, the founder of alibaba.com, also reiterates

"Today will be tough, tomorrow will be worse, but the day after will be wonderful, most of them quit tomorrow."

Success comes when you keep moving from failure to failure without losing hope.

CHAPTER - XIII
PROBLEMS LEADS TO PROSPERITY - FERRARI AND ILLAYARAJA

Any problem that occurs has some positive implication in it. This incident is not about who is right or who is wrong or who is weak or who is strong or who is good or who is bad, but what is right.

Friction breeds fast growth. When everything is smooth and when everything is in good terms, probably the industry becomes slow and saturated. Many get complacent about it. Out-of-the-box or extraordinary performance may not happen when everything is smooth.

Without the presence of Pepsi, Coke cannot experience such great growth. Without ICICI, HDFC cannot grow rapidly. If you truly desire growth, you need to encounter a problem. If you genuinely seek evolution, you should confront a tough emotional challenge.

In the book called 'Story of a Bonsai Manager', you will find that the Japanese want fresh fish. So there were challenges followed by solutions like.

- They started fishing and preserved it in ice. They found it was not good enough to taste.

- Then they stored it in a tank and made it live inside the ship. Still, it was docile, so they found the taste was not good enough.

- They kept a few sharks to keep them active. The active fish was tasty and catered fresh to the market. The challenges we face are like the sharks; they keep us active.

The action that you take to overcome the problem helps you to be healthy both in emotion and physical state. The chase of the shark makes the fishes inside the tank run for their life; this challenge made them healthy.

Similarly, we all know that Lamborghini was an engineer from a farmer family. He got jailed after losing in an Iranian war. He served his sentence repairing military vehicles. There he showed his 'mechanic skills'. Finally, he got released, came home, made a truck, made money, made huge money by selling his trucks. One fine day, a Ferrari got stuck on a highway. Since he was a mechanic, he took efforts to set it right. Also, he wrote a letter to Ferrari about the minor changes to make it better.

Ferrari replied that "A truck maker can better make trucks, we know how to make cars." This friction made

Lamborghini make cars, not just cars but something special, and 'Lamborghini cars' became a market leader in the same segment. Lamborghini is doing great; Ferrari is also great.

During the year 1990, friction between top Tamil directors and Ilaiyaraaja made Mani Ratnam bring a brand called A.R. Rahman. It made the market healthy, gave a new feel, and a lot of positive things happened in the music industry. It evolved due to friction; lack of time to work on many projects created friction between the music director and the movie director. Compromising on the re-recording of the project for which he had composed music was a bitter experience. Sometimes bitterness leads to something better. Henceforth, kindly understand that anything bitter will always have something better emerging from it.

'Problem leads to prosperity'

– Nat Cole King

Whose original name was Nathaniel Adams Coles. He was actually playing a musical instrument. When a drunken bar patron demanded that he should sing, he was startled since he was not a singer. Using the song *Sweet Lorraine* recorded in 1940, he sang the song. People heard Cole's vocal talent, they requested more vocal songs, and he obliged. He became a great singer, constructed a big theatre in the main place of America, and a most popular entertainer and prosperous entrepreneur. **Without the problem in the bar, he would neither have become a vocalist nor would have become a big entrepreneur.**

CHAPTER - XIV

SUNDAR.C AND THOUSAND KICKS OF BRUCELEE - PRINCIPLES OF MANAGEMENT

Application of Management Philosophy

When you read the philosophy of management, especially when you list out the principles of management, you will find one predominant thing.

"Do what you are good at."

— B.F. Skinner

A person who applied and proved their philosophy through his work was Mr. Sundar C.

Sundar C got an opportunity to work on a project called *Thalainagram*. He did a great job, was acknowledged as a hero, and since then chose to do a lot of hero roles in movies. He was very successful as a hero, and some of his songs became sensations in the state.

He did not get carried away by the success, and he did introspection. After introspecting well, he took a decision to say no to movies as a hero. This act is a lesson to many businessmen who keep wasting time doing something which is not their core competency. The veteran actor Shivakumar is a great artist and painter; still, he focused only on acting as a career.

Sundar C went back to his true trait, his inherent propensity of being a director, and came out with a movie called *Kalakalappu.*

The project sends a special and strong message to everyone **"I am back"**. We have seen many movies with horror and action to have a gripping screenplay. With humour, he had a gripping screenplay, a genuine masterpiece that can really change your mood and make you feel happy. Through this movie, he made people cry out of laughter.

Bruce Lee says that

> **"I Am Not Intimidated by a Person Who Knows 1000 Kicks but I Will Be Careful With a Person Who Has Practised One Kick 1000 Times."**

It simply says to choose your core game and inherent strong point and develop the discipline to stay grounded in the strength.

Be a master of your own craft, be proud of who owns that craft. Be proud of who you really are and do what naturally blossoms through you. Rather than artificially creating something to show you as something, put all your effort and focus on one thing in which you are a specialist. In the profession of a doctor, you will always find that the specialist is paid more than the general physician.

A business networking organisation called BNI tells us that

"Specific is Terrific."

After getting fired from Apple, when Jobs joined Pixar - all the 2000 employees slogged for hours on one project, *The Toy Story,* so Jobs asked the question to his team after rejoining Apple, "What is your Toy Story?"

"What is your one big thing? What is that one thing which you will be world-class?" This is called the power of one.

I would like to quote a small incident from the life of Picasso. Once he was walking in a market place, a lady asked him to draw a small piece of art. He drew that and gave it to her in a few seconds. She asked for its worth. He said it would be at least a few lakhs of rupees. "Oh! My God! You can draw a picture worth millions in a few seconds." Picasso smiled and said

> *"It took twenty-four years for me to draw a picture worth a million in a few seconds."*

Let me tell you - Why Specific is Terrific?

> **Specific Leads to Focus**
>
> **Focus Leads to Clarity.**
>
> **Clarity Leads to Mastery.**

Focus on your good talent and the natural flair and grow. Picasso did not try carpentry, singing, dancing, or writing stories; he remained as an artist to draw pictures. Hold your lens in the same place to create fire using sun rays.

> Don't be addicted to success at any cost
>
> **Become Successful by Being Who You Are Naturally.**

CHAPTER – XV
LEADING AT ANY LEVEL

Leadership Is Attitude, Not Designation. Not Only Heroes Are Leaders.

Leadership Lessons From

Y.G. Mahendran

Robo Shankar

Soori

Ramadas

Saranya Ponvannan

Lakshmi Ramakrishnan

The best place to learn leadership is from the example of certain characters who are very popular.

The amount of passion and diligence they put in for a particular part of the project defines the level of leadership. More than the personal glory, the passion to craft a better product and give the best customer experience, to serve the customer like a titan, they did a fabulous job even though their screen space was less. The amount of sacrifice was more than the self-interest. True world-class team players, small but significant professionals they are. In the movie called 'Yudhamsei', both Y.G. Mahendran and Lakshmi Ramakrishnan performed with high-voltage leadership. For the small screen time, yet significant in sacrificing their personal image to give a world-class project. Their feel for their professional excellence was higher than their personal identity in the movie. It's not how big the role was but how strongly you contribute to the given opportunity is the true leader's trait. Leadership is not in status but in their attitude to contribute.

Maari, a movie where Dhanush plays the lead role, even if seen after 10 years, when you look back, you would find the job done by Mr. Robo Shankar to be the epitome of his passion to deliver in every possible way and in every screen space given to him, making him a leader.

Though Sundarapandian was a movie with many positive aspects. Mr. Soori did a great job which will speak volumes about his passion for his role. The wit and variety he displayed were truly amazing. Similarly, Mr. Ramadas, in a movie called Mundasupatti, conducted with a lot of zeal and passion for the opportunity given. Needless to say, in any particular project, Mrs. SaranyaPonvannan delivers a full-throttle performance in all her movies for the past 10 years. If you try to remove her and replace any other person to substitute her role, I am sure the product will not be as good.

All the above things are possible for all. The above people achieved it all because of one characteristic. Can you guess? It is 'Gratitude'. They all have one thing in common. They are grateful for what they do and are passionate to contribute. They understand the worth of the opportunity and would like to reciprocate well by adding value to their project.

Leadership is not about position, title, and status. It is all about the quantum of love and respect you show towards your job. People have a misconception that designations and grades make them a leader. No, it's your character and attitude.

"The degree of gratitude inside reflects on the degree of leadership outside."

CHAPTER - XVI
ROCKER FELLER HABITS OF RAGAVA LAWRENCE

I underwent a Rockefeller habits training. Nowhere in my school or college was I told about Rockefeller. But the business concepts and the knowledge were profound to create a lasting impact, and I was amazed at the way you can accomplish things.

- Power of routine

- Daily discipline

- of life

- Going over the top

- DWIT - Do What It Takes

- Top-down flow of mission

- Huddle, meeting, and review

- Clarity on goals

Much more... It was a weak day training from morning to evening, though we had many learnings, one striking thing was very simple and not followed by the majority. Let me just give a small introduction about Rockefeller and his business success. If you can imagine the wealth of Warren Buffet and Bill Gates together, that would still be less compared to the wealth of Rockefeller. He was a tycoon who made people work for him and made commercial success out of the same. The Rockefeller family was an American industrial, political, and banking family that owns one of the world's largest fortunes. The fortune was initially made in the US petroleum industry during the late 19th and early 20th centuries by John D. Rockefeller and his brother William Rockefeller, primarily through Standard Oil. The family was also known for its long association with and control of Chase Manhattan Bank. The Rockefellers are considered to be one of the most powerful families, if not the most powerful family, in the history of the United States. In short, he accumulated the greatest amount of wealth through developing his business, and he had a management system which made it possible to do it. They call it Rockefeller habits and strategy.

I was inspired to see an actor and entrepreneur Lawrence Ragavendra could actually elucidate the principle and clearly made mileage out of it. One specific aspect of the training was greatly illustrated by him in a very clear manner, so that everyone could understand that learning and get benefit out of the same.

One of the Rockefeller strategies says

"When something works out to be successful, keep working on it again and against." Sounds simple. Still, let me explain.

When you do a project and if it becomes successful, kindly ensure and analyse what made it successful.

Get the client's feedback on what made it successful?

Get the team's feedback on what made it successful?

Find the factor and just do it bigger and better again and again, you will be more successful as an entrepreneur. Winning by design is the key to not just replicate but to improve success. Most of the time, we find people become so busy moving fast without introspection. When there is a specific success, find out which portion of it had given it and decode the act. With discipline and focus, do it again and again to keep getting more success.

Most of the time, we have a plan and execute it, and work hard to achieve the projected goal. We keep working on projects without looking at their success and the correct reasons for their success. Why do we miss it?

Urgency to show their creativity. Hankering in expressing their versatility. Not looking at the pertinent performance parameters. Not able to identify the core factor which impacts their success.

Not identifying the sweet spot of super success in business.

Not keen on going for a higher level of competency.

We undertake multiple projects.

We may have many different aspirations.

We may be keen on expressing everything.

Many winners are produced, but few champions in business. A winner will win occasionally, but a champion never loses; for him, winning is a habit. By optimising the parameters of excellence, you keep raising your brand power and client satisfaction. Be very certain and hit the bull's eye.

Just look at the evolution of Ragava Lawrence from being a dance master to becoming a producer of movies. The first movie called Muni - which had a combination of fun and fear factor as an integral part of the movie. It became a commercial success. It was a special surprise to see the success of a movie with a different type. The story does not end there. What made him the great and successful entrepreneur?

The first project was a humour and horror combo movie - Muni. He was patient enough to observe the success, learn, and identify the sweet spot of super success. Not just superficially seeing success, he saw the core reason for success; he was able to identify the fine parameter.

Imagine if you become successful with a movie, you would have so many varieties of storylines and so many different types of creators approaching you. All you need to do is prioritise what works.

What works, just work on it.

He identified that the fun component is really working out well. In part two of Muni-Kanchana, he ensured that he improved the fun part to 60% and horror to 40%. It was more successful than Muni. Have you ever heard of a part 2 doing better than part 1 in movie making? Here is Ragava Lawrence working on what works without trying to prove his point. Without confusing himself and the audience too much, he went ahead with the same with an improved combo. In part three, he improved the fun part to 70% and horror to 30%. Again, it became a good success for the company. He stayed committed on the ground and played his shot again and again with more vigour and power. He became MS Dhoni, and this equation (fun and horror combo) became his helicopter shot. Likewise, even though the percentage of time on horror was less, in terms of value addition, he kept the KAIZEN (constant improvement) moving on.

First part muni had one ghost with a fun element of lead.

Second part, Kanchana had three ghosts with a fun element of many,

The third part of Kanchana two had a plethora of multiple comic sequences.

All three parts had an aggressive song at the climax, a peppy song in the beginning, and a romantic song in the middle. He kept using the equation better and better. All he wanted was a good client experience. When you know how to contribute intelligently, you can do it again and again with more of your core strength.

So what is the simple lesson from this smart businessman?

When it works, just keep working on it.

Here, the importance must be given to identifying the core reason for success.

How can you identify the core reason for success?

Your analysis.

Your team analysis

Most importantly, your client feedback.

By collating everything and decoding it the correct way, you will find out the core parameter that contributed to the success.

Then start your project with the core parameter and execute it, emphasising more on the core parameter for success.

It may sound simple, yet how many of you know the core reason for your success?

Focus More on the Core Area.

More so, some of the corporates, after getting successful, end up doing something without optimising the success. They call it company policy and protocol. As creators, sometimes they get carried away by the success and don't even look out for the reasons for success.

What gave me success?

How can I make it bigger and better?

By answering the above two questions, don't waste time; just go and execute.

When it works, just work on it!

For success in business, do the following two

*Intelligent contribution.

*Inspire them to support.

CHAPTER - XVII

SOLID MESSAGE FROM SOUTH INDIAN DIRECTOR KHAKA KHAKA - GAUTHAM VASUDEV MENON

Two beautiful messages were very prominent and obvious which were elucidated in the movie called 'Khaka Khaka'. During my days of Civil Service preparation classes, I met a person next to me in the classroom of the Civil Service academy where I was attending. I had a candid conversation, I shared that my father was an IFS officer and he died when he was in service. So I would like to write this exam (quite reasonable) and I asked his reason for writing his exam. I was astounded by his reply. He did M.Tech from VIT, he aspired to become an IPS officer after watching the movie Khaka Khaka. Sounds funny, but really hard to believe. He told me that he wanted to live like Anbuchelvan. Such a great movie in the history of Tamil cinema which had a brilliant impact inside the theatre and even outside. I am too small to talk about the technicality and other extraordinary piece of work by the team but I am going to talk about two things which I teach people in my training particularly to young managers taking reference from the movie.

1. In Building Attitude - using a particular character as an example.

2. Building a mindset - using an event as an example

Let us look at the first one. **Attitude** and its power in our real world. During the encounters of the heinous criminals, one beautiful message was conveyed in a subtle manner. The most interesting part of the movie Khaka Khaka was the encounter by the four cops. The background score, gripping chase, and the first time they sizzled the encounter was a great treat to watch. We would witness all successful encounters by the cops. Energetic, vigilant, focused, agile, and spontaneous in their mode of operation.

The style in which they executed was amazing. Every encounter was full of zeal and passion except one. Just before one encounter, actor Daniel Balaji made a statement; in management terms, I call it the 'Mood Word' of the execution. We programme our minds with thoughts followed by words. The Neuro programming can be done using words, which will manifest in our real world.

The cop tells the following dialogue, "We are coming like supermen, what if the opponent was armed and starts to backfire."

In life, the mood plays a major role in the project that you do. After that particular dialogue, you will find that was the only time that the opponent will fire back at the cops, and the cop started bleeding, though not a big disaster, still a setback.

The bullet gets attracted to the cop who attracted the bullet into his body. "There are no accidents," as Master Shifu tells in the 'Kung Fu Panda' movie.

The cop did not get hit by the bullet by accident; he had set the 'Mood word' before execution, which resulted in the backfire. Thus, the mood and mental makeup determine the fate of every project.

You may practice for hours before the project, but how you set the mood before the execution defines the efficacy of the execution.

Before opening the door and firing, he had decided to lose by feeling and thinking desperately.

Winners play to win; losers play not to lose.

Winners play with faith; losers play out of fear.

Rather than choosing faith, he had chosen fear, which ended up in bleeding.

"Take care of your mood and it will take care of your mission."

Words can exist when there is a thought, so be careful in what you think. Our thought is first and foremost most important as there is a powerful thought wave which can be proven by EEG. Most importantly, whenever in life, you go to execute any project or crack any exam, take care of your psychology, your emotion, your 'thought word' - set it right and things will manifest from your mind as per your thought word. Everything happens twice in life - first in mind, second in life. In a day, we create 60,000 thoughts; the quality of this defines the quality of life.

Second Message

In my life, I have spoken one sentence whenever I open any new branch and also take my inspiration from the dialogue of the villain in *kakha kakha*.

In the movie, you will find the villain speaking a heroic dialogue. He not only looks good but also brands very differently and delivers things with class. The villain will come from Mumbai to Chennai to meet his brother. The local gangster would become calm due to the aggression shown by the cops. The villain, Pandia, from Mumbai comes with a refreshing attitude, not willing to get cowed by the act of cops, though his brother, who is a local gangster in Chennai, tells him to slow down the activities. Pandia could not get settled because he believes in the philosophy,

If you don't move forward, then you are moving backward, as there is nothing called neutrality in nature.

During an open fire encounter, Pandia never backed down or took his foot off the accelerator but walked forward with courage.

Keep moving forward in your business.

He delivers a wonderful message through his comment.

Height of Aggression.

Height of Attitude.

Height of courage.

Height of clarity.

I never forget this sentence when we start any new venture. Sometimes, the HR will wait for this statement since my session will not get completed without it. I gave a handwritten message to the leader who got promoted and moved to a new territory, new designation, new place, new team, and new task or even when they quit and move out of the country for projects. I smile at them and tell them to think like Pandia. Let me share the words of wisdom from Pandia.

"Wherever we go, we must rule the place. We must show the place who we are," in Gautham Menon's aggressive voice, it kindled fire.

The above words are the core values of his inner space.

The inner space of every human has two things

1. "I can"

2. "How can I?"

We keep giving power to both. It is like we create a terrorist group and we send the military to kill them. Sounds familiar? Sorry, I am not referring to any international politics, I just want to say that our inner space has these two components. Like Pandia feed only the 'I can' factor. The willpower should alone be groomed once the decision is taken.

Despite heavy opposition from the cops, the willpower of the villain was strong. The style with which he inspires people was magical.

He does not want to get stopped by the fear created by supercops. The aggression in his style and the way he faces the team.

The message he wants to convey through the action he takes is quick and brave. It's not just about being motivated, but the action that radiates motivation that makes the difference.

Pandya was a man of action. He demonstrated leadership not by just sounding aggressive, but by being aggressive in his actions.

What resonates inside comes out as action; the philosophy or dialogue resonated, hence he gave a run for the cops.

CHAPTER - XVIII

INNOVATION AND MAAN KARATE (MOVIE ON MOHAMED ALI)

Innovation and invention are two different things. Invention is creating a new thing whereas innovation is converting an existing invention into a good or service which adds value.

If the above definition is very complicated and if you find it too hard to know the difference between invention and innovation, let me put things simply. Poori masala may be an invention (poori with potato sabji as a combination) product and a suitable support system to present it.

Dosa, sambar may be an invention (Dosa with onion stew as a combination) product and a suitable support system to present it. When they take a decision to make a masala dosa, it is nothing but innovation.

Innovation can be achieved by amalgamating two or more existing ideas and themes. Not creating new products but providing a new experience to the end user by combining existing products.

The movie 'Godfather' was presented as the movie 'Nayagan'. 'Mahabharata' was presented as the movie

'Thalapathy'. Mouna Raagam was presented as 'Raja Rani'.

The masterpiece of Vijayakanth was presented as 'Their' by Vijay. Similarly, we can find the great boxer Muhammad Ali's historic victory story over Sonny Liston. This history was presented as a movie called 'Maan Karate'. Where the style of Usain Bolt and flavours of Sivakarthikeyan, humours were amalgamated to get into a product which added value to clients.

Go to YouTube and type "The fight that shook the world". You will find a video and a small story followed by emotional narration by an individual. Muhammad Ali acting smart and playing a prank with the psychology of Sonny.

Sunny challenges to kill him in the ring. But the only commercial element in the movie Maan Karate is that you can't win a professional without practice. But Muhammad Ali speaks to the media to disturb Sunny emotionally.

"If you bet on Sunny, you will lose your money."

Internally, Mohamed Ali was not at all confident. So he used words like

"I am the greatest. I am the champion."

While practicing on the punch bag, he found it hard to convince himself before convincing the world.

This shows the power of words. This proves the power of the law of attraction in life also. We should tell ourselves, "I am the greatest."

The idea to create a theme where they can accommodate the hero Shivakarthikeyan who behaves crazily in front of the media and plays with the ego of the opponent.

The climax was epitomised by the essence of Rocky

"Life is not about how hard you hit. Life is all about how hard you get hit and move forward."

Shiva Karthikeyan gets hit to the maximum and still endures to stand up.

Adding the superb flavour of Chandragiri forest with the IT employees made the drama very interesting, and the love story was also fabricated to fit inside the plot.

Adding icing to the cake was the depiction of Usain Bolt's style to the character called Maan Karate Peter. The net result was a super success. I felt that proper practice and honour to the opponent must be preserved. I felt no one should be humiliated. Still, I enjoyed the way it was packed and presented.

Wow, what an innovation to make movies.

CHAPTER - XIX
COLONAL SANDERS AND MOTTAI RAJENDRAN

Some people think that sixty is a retirement age and after which they should not work or stop working at that age. They don't understand that age is just a number compared to the willpower of a human being. Age is nothing, so nothing can stop you from growing ahead in your life. As you become old, you get more matured; you may develop the suitable knowledge which may end up giving you the greatest power of success in your life.

Losing money, losing family, losing job, losing hope to live only with a recipe. Mr. Col Sanders, at the age of 65, built a billion-dollar company called KFC. After becoming a senior citizen, Sanders became a well-known businessman. It is not a small success in his professional growth; it is a big leap, a huge giant leap in his life. Be ready always; when opportunity meets you, you should be ready to go for a big bang and make your lasting impact in life.

'When opportunity meets preparation that is called luck'. A person who strived hard to survive ended up creating a charitable trust 'Sanders Charitable Organisation', based in Canada.

I would like to compare the career growth of Sanders with that of Mottai Rajendran. This bald-headed actor, who was introduced in the movie called 'Naankadavul' as a villain, is fit and fine with six packs at the age of sixty. He explored his talent in acting.

Became the most sought-after actor in Tamil cinema by his presence. People were happy, and he kept moving from strength to strength. He does not chase success. He enjoyed his work, and success kept pouring at his feet.

Irrespective of the size of the project, both Vijay and Ajith had Mottai Rajendran as a part of their movie. He became an inevitable part of any successful project for his inherent talent and eagerness to act. He jumps at the opportunity provided to him and gives his best possible effort. He is not bothered about the result. As ghost Gopal, he did a great job in a horror movie. His unique voice cannot be easily replicated. He used it to amuse us by singing a song in a movie climax (kadhaanayagan). Hilarious, finding the right way to use you to amuse the world is brilliant. The right way of placing your uniqueness is a brilliant art.

He is the Sanders of the Tamil comedy world. It's a pleasure to watch him take crafting new kinds of roles in different kinds of movies.

He sculpted himself as a great comedian.

CHAPTER - XX
ARAVINDA SWAMY AND EAGLE PHILOSOPHY

The childhood wonder for many might be the movie 'Roja'. Being a great new face actor with a very neat and decent look, Aravind Swamy went on to become one of the most popular Tamil movie actors. Getting featured in a movie is tough. Getting directed by Mani Ratnam is still tougher. Creating an everlasting impression among the audience is the toughest job. This man with his inborn charm was able to make it big. Not just big but a huge fan base in his life at a very early age. It was really hapless that he had health issues and needed to take care of his business for obvious reasons, swerved out of movies for a long time. All of a sudden, he was out of the acting market. A real disappointment for all the fans who admired him for years. Now let me connect this with a beautiful story of an eagle.

The story of the eagle was quite popular. Very inspiring to read the story of the eagle. I feel passionate to explain the same to you. Some common facts about eagles we must know.

An eagle can have powerful vision for two kilometres. The ability to have such a powerful vision for such a large distance.

Unlike other birds which glide with the direction of the wind and make the glide easy, it generally stands against the wind on the mountain edge to strengthen its arms. It glides above the cloud and is not disturbed by the showers and turbulence. One strange habit of the eagle is it pushes its own baby from the top of the cliff to enable its ability to take flight and live strong or die. Do you know an eagle can even catch a deer on the ground? An eagle is not an ordinary bird; it is known for its strength and uniqueness.

When the eagle becomes 40, it takes a different decision. It understands that its feathers become weak, nails not strong enough, and beak not hard enough to support its hunt. It voluntarily plucks off its feathers, breaks its nails and beak. It will starve for 90 days without food, then it rejuvenates with the vigour and power it possessed before 30 years. With the same power and strength, it will live for the rest of life. It's almost a rebirth for the eagle.

After a long break from movies and acting, Mr. Aravind Swamy came back in a movie called 'Thani Oruvan' with a similar power of the eagle. Not just physically but mentally empowered with a fire to take on this industry by storm again. Get ready, folks! Happy news that he not just survived the tough time. He is stronger than before. More clear, extremely matured, focused on his acting career.

If you are going through a tough time, think of his performance in Thani Oruvan. It's not just a re-entry. It's a message for all of us to believe in the power of hope. The power of positive expectation. He proves that tough times will not last but tough people last long. They prove stronger than the hurdles they face in their life. They break the barriers with a tough attitude. He did not stay away from movies; he built a stronger version of himself. It was not hibernation but high-voltage creation. Arvind Swamy is a real-life example of the eagle philosophy. It's never hopeless at any stage; everyone can have a wonderful comeback if they work on themselves.

CHAPTER - XXI
VIKRAM AND PHOENIX PHILOSOPHY

It would be a criminal offence to hide the great comeback of the man with iron will, Vikram (or) Kenny.

He met with a great tragedy in his life. Suffered a wound and got bedridden for months as the way the doctor proclaims in the movie 'Dhil'. He was certified that he could not return to normal life. They even intimated that he may not be able to walk. After that, he became fit physically, mentally, and, most importantly, psychologically. His mental stamina and passion to push harder are equivalent to that of a samurai warrior.

He had a small breakthrough as a hero during his early age, but after that, he strived hard to create a big and lasting impact in different roles. The real manifestation happened when he did the project called 'Sethu'. Director Bala is another great warrior with a genuine motto to give good cinema to society.

What is so special about Vikram and what is so special about the 'Sethu' movie. Generally, movies will run for 100 days. But to buy and distribute the movie 'Sethu', it took more than 100 shows to convince the person to take up the business. People were not ready to buy the movie and were quite apprehensive about its commercial success.

The movie was so unique, and Vikram had a wonderful comeback after overcoming all the tough times of his life. Sethu ran to full houses for months, and Vikram established his great identity. After that, he dominated the industry for years with his excellent acting skills. He dared to put all his heart into the movie and wanted to be the best actor ever to have lived on this planet.

He cannot compromise on anything for his profession; he can compromise any other thing for his profession. Whatever projects come his way, he throws himself with all his heart into the project. When you rewind his life 25-30 years back, other than Vikram, no one else would have believed that he would become so great in his career.

The mythology says that the phoenix bird rises from the ashes and moves towards the sun again and again. We need to call Mr. Vikram the phoenix of Tamil cinema.

He is fearless to do any kind of role. Loves to give his best abilities at all stages of life. A lot of time he has risked his own life.

Once Ratan Tata was travelling in a car that got punctured, and all the officials who accompanied him got out and started to relax in the nearby shop for refreshment while the tyre was being fixed.

All of a sudden, they found that Ratan Tata was missing. They searched for him everywhere but could not find him. By chance, one person saw him helping the driver to change the stepney. He rolled up his shirt cuffs. While others were thinking that it was the job of a driver, the leader rolled his sleeves and changed the tyre.

"To be a master, you should serve." - Jesus Christ

When people on the sets of a movie called Samurai had a snag and a few crew members were in danger, Vikram did not move out of the spot in a caravan or luxury car to just save himself. He went out into the forest hanging over a rope to save his team members. I find so many modern finicky heroes assume that being a hero means we are superior. But Vikram is such a simple soul who gets into servant leadership during the hardship. It's not a question of whether the movie was a hit or a flop, but the attitude that you demonstrate as a human toward your team matters. Vikram acted like Ratan Tata.

 # Your attitude matters #
#Rise high every time you fall down#

CHAPTER - XXII
VIVEK AND THE LAUGHING BUDDHA - THE PLAYFUL ZEN MONK OF TAMIL CINEMA

Comedy is a serious business maybe, I always feel the most intelligent of human beings get into the comedy business.

The way they think, feel, say, and do is really remarkable.

I want to tell you the story of Laughing Buddha. He was a playful, fun-loving, kind, and generous master. He moved from one town to another spreading happiness.

He handed out sweets and gifts to little children from the sack of the bag he carried and then dropped the bag down and laughed at the sky. Then people around him also laughed as well. That shows his job is done. He will pick up the bag and start his journey to the next village or town. A method of spreading happiness and enlightenment.

His message 'Giving' – The more you give, the more you receive.

Big Problems are like the bag that you carry, just put it down and laugh at it. Because whether you laugh or cry, the problem bag is not going to change. With laughter, the problem looks smaller and easier to handle.

When you laugh, your body produces positive hormones. A Zen monk, even during his time of death, asked his disciples to burn him quickly after he dies.

This was against Zen Buddhism, but still they did this. Surprisingly, he packed his body full of crackers which burst out and made people laugh even at his death. That was his mission.

"Drop your bag and be happy."

Great Buddhist intelligence, Great Zen Buddhist with a noble mission.

People call Vivek the China Kalaivanar, but I would like to treat him as a Buddhist monk who was very simple and profound.

His humour made people laugh at their own stupidity and transform into a better being. His humour was sensible and also sensational.

The choice of words and his body language was in beautiful sync, which made a lasting impression on the people's minds.

He continued to do his job despite a tragedy which is far worse than anything. His son died due to an unexpected fever. It is tough to describe the feeling of his absence. Having the memory of his son in his heart, he was working like a Zen monk, spreading happiness.

I am happy to give

I am happy to make you happy.

I am committed to making you happy at all costs.

A great salute to this Zen monk of Indian cinema. He was intelligently interesting and interestingly intelligent. He was so spontaneous. A humourist par excellence.

For people who give personal reasons for not performing in their profession, they should think of Vivek and get back to action.

At any cost

In any situation

Do your duty

With utmost sincerity.

He led a life as an embodiment of commitment to excellence. Moreover, he has an exceptional quality of appreciating the good in all politicians from all political parties. He can appreciate them with all his heart and humour. In this world where people are curious to say bad things about others, he was spreading a positive message about all leaders of all parties. Young people like us should learn from him.

He also addressed social problems and made people think about the unwanted stigma that troubled and hampered the growth of our society. He was very clear in castigating superstition without disrespecting religion. It requires intelligence and the right intention to do it.

CHAPTER - XXIII

WHAT DO YOU DO WITH YOUR WEAKNESS - LESSONS FROM THALA AJITH, THALAPATHY VIJAY, MOHAN RAJ

Sometimes human beings become so sensitive about their weaknesses and worry a lot about them and tell themselves that nothing can be done about it.

They become defensive about it and may live and die with that. On the other hand, there are people who turn back and move towards the so-called weakness. They behave so hard and brutal towards their weakness. They behave very tough.

Imagine Luz Long, the paralysed girl at the age of 13 makes a statement: "I want to be the fastest woman on the planet."

Failing miserably in her initial days, she struggled hard to walk with braces, then started to run. She came last in the competition, then began to run fast. In the next few years, she finally made her way to the Olympics and created a record.

Imagine composing music after losing the ability to hear.

Now I am talking about Beethoven.

What is so special about the above two people?

Luz Long could aspire to become a singer or author. A paralysed girl may think of singing, writing poetry, or mastering another instrument, but her willpower was different.

Beethoven can compose poems and paint pictures.

But their decision to break down their barriers was very rare.

How is it possible?

They accepted their weakness. They decided to start from where they are. This acceptance alone gives them the courage.

Acceptance leads to maturity. Maturity leads to calmness.

Calmness leads to a balanced mind. A balanced mind leads to strength. Strength leads to creativity. Creativity leads to success.

They moved out of their comfort zone and broke their barriers.

In the Tamil cinema industry, around 60% of the stakes of the fan club are shared by Illayathalapathi Vijay and Thala Ajith, with both sharing approximately 30% each.

Looking back to the 1990s when both of them were trying their best to create their impression in the Tamil movie industry.

Vijay was trying hard with his normal complexion, and his dance movements were commented on as so mechanical in his initial days. He was made fun of for the mechanical way of dancing without any grace. People laughed at his dance and made comments that he could amount to nothing in the market. His dance movements were very mechanical. He was trying hard, moving hands and legs fast and forcefully without any sense of grace or love towards dance.

10 years down the line, during the 2001 to 2010, he made a great turnaround. Especially in the movie 'Youth', the 'Aalthotaboopathy' song could speak volumes of his grace.

Now he is regarded as the most graceful dancer in the Tamil movie industry.

He accepted his flaws and worked on his dance; now it has got refined, defining a true class of excellence.

Similarly, Thala Ajith had a tough entry into the industry, but when he spoke about sentiment and when he cried in the movie 'Poovellam Kaettupar' as 'chella chella', it sounded not good to many, and as usual, people started to comment on his voice.

Then he took on many strategic, aggressive, and antiheroic roles which gave him a break.

Now in the movie 'Veeram' he makes a rumble with his bass voice. *Yenn ala thodanumna yennathaandi* (meaning, if you want to touch my people you need to touch me first) - The theatre reverberates in energy, you get goosebumps. Yes, he accepted his shortcomings and found good roles to suit him and get the best out of him.

To convert any weakness into strength, focus on the feedback and accept it. Director Mohan Raja made 'Thanioruvan' where he wanted to be the best and faced the truth brutally. He pulled himself up like Muhammad Ali in a boxing ring, converting the myth that he lacks creativity and does only remake movies. Known for his success with copying or remaking Telugu scripts.

Silenced his critics with his movies 'Thani Oruvan' and 'Velaikkaran'. Look at the belief in himself. See how he converted negativity into positivity.

Accept your true trait today, then courage will blossom automatically.

CHAPTER – XXIV
LATERAL THINKING – EDWARD DE BONO AND SANTHANAM

The wonderful movie called 'Shiva Manasula Shakthi' was known for its power and freshness. Santhanam worked at his best, coming up with quick and apt sense of humour. I sense the hidden message from the book called *6 Thinking Hats* written by Edward de Bono (the father of lateral thinking). In that book, he tells that different perspectives should be taken by wearing different hats, thinking and feeling in a particular way.

In an organisation, he recommended people to have different options for a case study. Evaluate different options by making everyone think in a particular direction. Maturity is to understand the different aspects and see things from another's point of view. It is a high-level of maturity to think. Santhanam in the movie says, "*ovvoru manushanukkum ovvoru feeling*". Every individual has a different feeling, and every individual has a unique feeling. Rather than confronting others' feelings, maturity is to understand the different feelings.

Like the crux of the book called 'The Immortals of Meluha'.

People are different, not bad. Suryavanchi and Chandravanchi are different, and not bad.

There is a difference in beauty; there is beauty in the difference, understand.

In the book 'Men are from Mars and women are from Venus', we can see the power of acknowledging the difference. 'Ovvoru manushanukkum ovvoru feeling'. Also, I would like to reiterate the incident from the book, 'MADE IN JAPAN'.

Where the founder of the company *SONY* due to some difference of opinion between him and one more key person on the board in a particular discussion, the other person loses his cool and decides to quit by moving out. Immediately, Akio Morita approached him and told him, "You should have differences to balance. Any organisation should have different views which will balance the risk in decision-making."

Everyone should not just say yes to every decision. We should have someone who thinks the other way so that every decision will be balanced. The calculated risk can be taken in this regard.

In his legendary Stephen Covey book 'Seven Habits of Highly Effective People', you will find the habit: "Seek first to understand than to be understood."

It was practised in one of the tribal groups to resolve disputes by a method in which they give a bamboo to one person (one among the disputed party). He needs to speak for the opposite party. Then, to another person, the bamboo was passed, and a similar exercise will be encouraged. Respect the differences, kindly understand (ovvoru manushanukkum ovvoru feeling). We can have differences in opinion, but greater understanding will evolve when we develop the maturity to see the conflict and, more so, the exact place where the deviation happens. In your life, whenever there is a conflict, just close your eyes and say

Even Swami Vivekananda was humiliated for his dress outside of the country because their sympathies are limited to the way people dress. When he spoke to them in English, they felt ashamed. But Swami Vivekananda did not hate them; he made them understand that he is different, not bad.

Ovvoru manushanukkum ovvoru feeling

Different Not Bad.